RESTLESS LEGS SYNDROME (RLS):

9 WAYS TO RELIEVE DISTRESSING SYMPTOMS AND AID BETTER SLEEP

L J HUDSON

WORSFOLD-WHITE PUBLISHING

CONTENTS

Just for you!

Follow this link here to download your own PDF copy of Eight Air Purifying Plants to Aid sleep.

I would like to dedicate this volume to all the sufferers of Restless Leg Syndrome, their families, partners, and GP's. It isn't just one person who suffers it is all of those mentioned. I hope to be able to help at least one person with their journey with RLS.

Lisa

INTRODUCTION

Over the years I have had considerable pain and discomfort from my legs, especially when I was trying to rest or settle down for the night. To begin with, I didn't have it every night or even every week, but I hated it! I think I was only 18 when I asked my mum about it even mentioning that I thought I had restless legs but all she said was she had it as well, but it usually went away during the night. She did not consider it all that much of a problem! I should not be concerned or worried about it. She brushed it off, she was like that! That was all very well for her, but it was driving me crazy when I had it.

I was training as a nurse in Plymouth from 1985 to 1988 when it increased in severity and started to become more of an issue. I spent long hours on my feet, and of course, being a student, often went out and partied until late too. It was considered the law! I noticed that when I had a very long day like this, my legs started to 'play up' and I had to resort to Paracetamol or Ibuprofen to help. Thankfully, in those days these worked reasonably well, and I could control the discomfort to a degree. Often it would only last a couple of hours and then go, so at this point, it was not that disruptive.

I did ask my doctor about it, but in the mid- 1980s knowledge about Restless Legs Syndrome (RLS) was very minimal and he only suggested I continue with the over-the-counter medicines (OCM). I remember I left his office disappointed that he had not even diagnosed what this problem was. I used some of my spare time to do a little research on the subject but was unable to find a lot about it in the hospital library. In those days, I did not have the luxury of the internet as we do today, and my searches were long and generally unfruitful.

So, I coped with it back then and thought nothing more of it. It was an inconvenience I suffered from, and I just got on with it.

Fast forward to somewhere in the mid- 2000s, and life has moved on. I was then a single mother to my son and had seen off two marriages. I was working hard to support the two of us, our pets, and pay the interest on my mortgage. At this time, I was still nursing and working in a radiotherapy outpatient department, spending long hours walking up and down the unit and the hospital every day. I was noticing that my legs began to react badly and the RLS worsened. I found it hard to get comfortable and settle at night, my legs felt hot, then cold. They hurt, felt tight like I was cramping, but did not quite get to that stage of full cramp, and worse, I had the uncontrollable urge to keep moving them. Some nights, staying in bed was not an option. My sleep cycle was beginning to suffer badly at this point; paracetamol and ibuprofen were not as effective, and the sleep deprivation started to get to me. I did not realize how much until I met my current husband who actually cared about me and my son. I began to rely on him, because he allowed me to, but it was like letting off a pressure valve, and I reacted with a bit of a wobble at work causing me to run out on an incredibly busy clinic which I had been coordinating. That Friday was just too demanding on me when I was fatigued and running on empty. I had already sent three patients by ambulance to our main hospital and a further two needed to go as well. The fire alarm went off just at the busiest of times, and to top it all, at one point, I had about five people all talking at me and wanting something urgent. It was no wonder I threw my hands up in the air, told them I couldn't cope anymore, and ran off into a spare office to sob my heart out.

That mental breakdown resulted in my being off work for five months whilst I got my head back in order. I was a mess. I found it hard to concentrate, was generally depressed, felt groggy from the medications I had been prescribed, and had the double whammy of neither my head nor my legs allowing me to get restful sleep. There was still little help from my doctor for the RLS and once again I just coped.

I did eventually return to work but left that job due to the stresses and decided to take some time off away from any work. It coincided with a family holiday to Florida and Disney. Whilst I was there, I thought for a long time about my future and finally decided that perhaps due to my fragile mental health and the problems I was having with the RLS, I would be better taking a more sedentary role doing something else entirely.

Eventually, after around six months, I found a role at our local police department working within the vetting unit. I loved it! However, I was now sat for almost eight hours a day behind a computer. I did not realize at the time this was not the wisest of moves to have made. Within a few years of being there and several moves into different offices of various levels of draftiness, I noticed that I had to get up frequently from my desk and pace the office trying to relieve the cramping, crawling pains starting in my legs. Great! Now it was getting to me in the daytime!

I began to research; Google became my friend. When I had five full nights of absolutely no sleep, I made a doctor's appointment in desperation. I turned up to the appointment with reams of information about studies, approved drugs, and treatments for RLS. I even had my speech rehearsed and ready to go. To my great surprise, I didn't need it! He listened to me, asked a few questions about what I expected him to do about it, and then without any prompting or hesitation, he prescribed my first medication. That night, I had the best night's sleep ever, boy, did I need it!

Since then, I have researched even more and tried quite a few ways of dealing with the symptoms of RLS. This was further driven by necessity as around two years ago, I was diagnosed with Fibromyalgia. Suddenly, the penny dropped and a lot of what I had been experiencing, fell into place. The relationship between the two conditions is well documented and I became interested in how I could help myself to cope with both.

The Fibromyalgia aspect of my health is likely to be a whole other book, but I feel that I must share with my fellow sufferers everything I have discovered along my journey with RLS. Those of you who have coped for years as I have may have stumbled across much of what is contained here; but there will be those of you who are new to a diagnosis of RLS and are only just beginning to understand how to cope with it and try to alleviate the symptoms of this distressing disorder.

No two of us will experience the same symptoms. Personally, I don't get the involuntary jumpiness of my legs as some do. It is more a tightness in my calf which radiates down to my ankle and then up to my thigh. The sensation is painful and creepy crawly. I need, no, have to move my legs constantly for relief, and - often. If in bed, I find I need to stand up and rock until my drugs kick in, or whichever pain relief I have handy, is beginning to work. Sometimes nothing works at all! The damn drugs don't work, and I find myself pacing through the house, often in tears due to exhaustion and the fatigue caused by my Fibro and the RLS. I just want to sleep, and I can't due to these bloody legs! Sleep is not all that much to ask for, is it?

It is in all our interest to try to do the best we can for ourselves. Like many, I rely on the medications I have had prescribed to help me cope with the symptoms, but so many times, this is not enough. I fully believe that we should do everything in our power to find alternative therapies to complement the treatments given by our doctors and be seen to be trying to help ourselves.

So, with this in mind, I felt that I wanted to share the knowledge I have gained with others, to help them cope too. So long as it does not interfere with the current treatment regimens you are on, there is nothing wrong giving something else a go. I can't confess to all of them working for me, but some have, with varying success. I can say that my sleep is generally much better, and I am not so badly affected by the symptoms of RLS at present. That isn't to say that it doesn't drive me up the pole sometimes!

So, what follows is not a scientific treatise designed to confuse or befuddle, but I shall describe what RLS is, signs and symptoms, drug treatments, alternative therapies, and I hope, loads of helpful stuff to give you more than a fair crack at coping well with it. Maybe even the 'old hands' will find something new to help. I'll keep the science and research stuff to an acceptable level, and hopefully, in terms, we all understand. I must emphasize that I am not an 'expert' on the condition, the only expertise I can claim is that I suffer and so I know.

I do also touch a little on the darker side of this condition. I am aware for some, sleep deprivation, pain, and depression can become overwhelming. This can lead to thoughts of self-harm and suicide, so there is a chapter at the end which covers this too. After all, dark thoughts are within us all, I would be lying if I denied I had not had them.

I am convinced the contents of this book will help to improve the quality of sleep for you to some degree, and I am very excited about this project because I see it as an opportunity to help you. By giving you the knowledge, you require, I hope you will have new, positive experiences. I might never meet you in my life, and you might never meet me. Still, I feel privileged that I can have the opportunity to help you with this guide.

Please read on, I hope you find something within the pages to help you. If you do, then I have succeeded in my goal.

Lisa

1

WHAT IS RESTLESS LEGS SYNDROME (RLS)?

This part of the book is a little bit long-winded. However, I feel it is very important one understands the condition we suffer from. Bear with me, it does get more interesting further along the way.

RLS *is* a medical condition. It *is* real and has been categorized as such. It was first described by Thomas Willis (1865) and later further described by Karl-Axel Ekbom (1945) and so the condition is also known as Willis-Ekbom disease. The date of Karl-Axel Ekbom's birthday has been commemorated as Restless Legs Syndrome awareness day. The first of these days was 23 September 2012.

There is an acronym URGE which defines the major components of RLS:

> **U** – Urge to move the limbs also associated with an unpleasant or uncomfortable sensation
> **R** – Resting makes it worse
> **G** – Gets better when up and walking around
> **E** – Evening worsening

The condition affects seven to eleven percent of the population in European countries and around ten percent in the USA and affects more women than men. It is a sensorimotor, neurological, and sleep disorder and the symptoms tend to appear when one is trying to sleep or rest. This forces the urge for one to get up and move one's limbs which gives only temporary relief. Restless legs can start at any age, but symptoms can worsen as one gets older. Pregnant women and in their last three months of pregnancy also seem to suffer the condition, but the good news is that it is known to gradually go away soon after delivery. It is also the most common disorder which causes sleep disruption.

Pregnancy

As mentioned above, pregnancy is often the cause of RLS. Some women experience the symptoms, especially in the last trimester. However, the symptoms often go away within about a month of delivery. Research has shown that women who suffer during pregnancy might predispose to having it later in life. However, it has been noted that not all pregnant women will experience RLS. It is a bit of a mystery as to why.

What Are the Symptoms?

The symptoms of RLS are generally the most severe in middle-aged people. It can be difficult for doctors to recognize and diagnose this syndrome, especially when the symptoms are mild or rarely occur. In the past there was often clinical scepticism as to whether RLS *was* an actual illness. Some clinicians believed it to be 'all in the head' of the patient, or even 'all in the legs' referring to vascular disorders. The condition has been diagnosed incorrectly, doctors believing there was no effective treatment, or the condition was completely mismanaged. However, it *is* common, and it *is* distressful.

A constant, overwhelming and uncontrollable urge to move the legs is the most obvious symptom of RLS, however, there are other accompanying characteristics that can make one suspect RLS.

Sensations usually begin when one has been sitting or lying down for an extended time, such as when at a desk, in an airplane, car, or movie theatre. One will have the urgent need to get up and move around. It will only happen occasionally, and the sensations will not be so serious in the early stages. This is one of the major reasons why sufferers don't feel they need to see a doctor at this point or conversely, don't feel the doctor will believe their symptoms.

Those who have RLS notice when they move their legs by stretching, jiggling, pacing, or walking that the uncomfortable feeling they have reduces. The sensations will disappear when one does any form of exercise in most cases, but it is likely to come back, especially if it is a chronic issue.

It is usually during the evening when one is likely to notice the symptoms. One feels normal during the day, likely because one is active and could almost assume that the symptoms are gone until getting home in the evening and trying to relax. Symptoms worsen at this point, and this is why RLS disrupts sleep so often.

RLS has an association with a more common condition known as Periodic Limb Movement Disorder (PLMD). In fact, over eighty percent of people with RLS have PLMD. Characteristically, one's limbs fidget, twitch and kick through the night while sleeping. This could be severe enough to actually harm the person you sleep with and rip through bedsheets! It can emulate the symptoms of RLS, making it hard to distinguish between the two.

These unpleasant sensations in the legs or feet are usually either on one or both sides of the body. In some cases, they might start from one side of the body before moving to the other. Though less common, the sensations can affect the arms, chest, or even your head.

The ways sufferers of RLS describe their symptoms range widely as described below:

- Creeping
- Crawling
- Itching
- Throbbing
- Painful
- Tight
- Aching
- Pulling
- Pins and needles
- Burning
- Uncomfortable
- Stretching
- Tingling
- Heavy
- Tugging
- gnawing

In some cases, sufferers of this condition describe how they feel the symptoms to be challenging. However, the most common description of the condition is that it has a similarity to muscle cramp or numbness. The symptoms differ from one person to another and tend to fluctuate in severity. It is often reported that the symptoms disappear sometimes but may come back later.

What Are the Causes Of RLS?

Research on RLS is still ongoing. As of now, researchers cannot provide an exact explanation regarding the reason people experience these mild to intolerable symptoms. Genetics may play a crucial role. The reason for the feasibility of this explanation is that nearly half of those experiencing RLS, also have a family member with this condition. Other plausible causes include:

Chronic Conditions

There are two types of RLS, primary and secondary. Primary is also called idiopathic RLS having no clear cause, and often running in families. Secondary RLS occurs in connection with predisposing disorders or chronic conditions, such as:

- Multiple Sclerosis (MS)
- Diabetes
- End-stage kidney disease (ESKD)
- Iron deficiency
- Varicose veins
- Parkinson's disease
- Thyroid disease
- Peripheral neuropathy
- Spinal cord conditions
- Fibromyalgia

It is always better for one to have a medical check-up rather than to assume one knows exactly what is wrong. When doctors treat chronic disease, one might also be indirectly treating the RLS. Therefore, it is in one's best interest to depend on professional medical guidance.

Heredity

There are times that RLS may be due to genetics, especially if the symptoms manifest before the age of 40. It is not uncommon that a parent, sibling, or grandparent has experienced the symptoms themselves and have done for many years. If this is the case one can assume a family connection.

Lifestyle

Lifestyle factors like smoking and alcohol intake can trigger the symptoms of RLS. They can also make the symptoms worse. Experts also suggest that those who are fond of excessive consumption of tobacco, alcohol, and caffeine are at risk of experiencing the twitching and kicking associated with this neurological disorder.

Complications of RLS

It is known that RLS does not lead to other serious medical conditions. Still, symptoms can range from barely noticeable to incapacitating. It can make it virtually impossible for one to sleep, thereby interfering with one's quality of life. Other factors may also impact daily routine.

Fatigue

The importance of having consistent quality sleep cannot be overemphasized. Sleep helps to repair and restore the body's damaged cells and tissues. It also makes one fresh and ready for the tasks of a new day. When one does not have enough sleep, feelings of being jaded and fatigued can affect the ability to perform normal tasks. Repeatedly poor sleep can affect mental and physical health over time.

Poor Performance

How can one perform at the peak of one's powers when much of the night is spent experiencing uncomfortable sensations in one's legs or some other parts of the body? The fatigue and lack of sleep can interfere with focus during the day, especially when one's mind keeps drifting to other thoughts. One can be less effective or efficient because capability will be diminished.

It gets worse when involved in activities that require more concentration such as writing, calculous, or research. When carrying out these kinds of jobs, it is crucial that one feels alert so that simple mistakes are not made at work. It might be obvious when as part of a team tasked with making decisions within a company, one's contributions might not be as significant as normal due to lack of sleep. Professional relationships may be affected and there could be a chance of job loss if the situation is allowed to continue.

Breakdown In Professional and Personal Relationships

No boss likes to find employees sleeping whilst on duty. Neither will colleagues want to continue to cover for you. However, one might not be able to help it when quality sleep is lacking. Of course, this is in an extreme situation and a worst-case scenario, but it may occur.

All the above could also hamper personal relationships, such as a marriage or partnership. Family members may notice a lack of interaction at home with chores, children, and the logistics of running a busy household and one may be accused of being lazy especially if the situation persists. The situation must be explained to them, if they aren't already aware, to avoid ruining such relationships.

Depression

Note that depression is a mood disorder. So, it's not just an occasional feeling one has when one has had a bad day. We all have days or situations that make us occasionally unhappy. This doesn't mean that one is really suffering from depression. Depression is a consistent feeling of sadness that can lead to social withdrawal and the inability to enjoy any activity. It is a severe mental issue and a leading factor in self-harm and even suicide at its peak. According to the World Health Organization (WHO), depression is one of the most prevalent psychological conditions affecting millions of people around the world.

Depression may be inevitable when one is continually unable to sleep and finding it difficult to cope with daily activities. Remember my reference to suddenly needing to leave my post and go and cry in an office? I did not realise it then, but clearly, I had depression and it is no wonder! The cumulative impact of RLS on various aspects of one's life also seriously impacts one's quality of life. Therefore, don't wait until RLS pushes one to a desperation point before doing something about it. Meeting a therapist that can help with depression will not help in the long run if the sleep problem is not first dealt with.

If you notice all or most of these symptoms happening to you, act before it gets out of hand. It is normal if you feel that the doctor might not take you seriously when you decide to seek medical attention, however, doctors have a duty of care to attend to you. So, do not assume you will not be believed or made to feel stupid. As I mentioned, RLS can interfere with one's sleep affecting quality of life. Therefore, you must seek solutions to this problem before the symptoms become too severe.

2

CURRENT APPROVED MEDICATIONS

The governing bodies which authorize the use of medications are the Medicines and Healthcare products Regulatory Agency (MHRA) in the UK and the US Food and Drug Administration (FDA). Drugs are generally authorized for use for a specific condition; however, it is widely known that one drug successful for a specific condition may also be helpful in controlling another. When this happens, the drug is being used "off book". Many of the drugs currently used in the treatment of RLS are these so called "off book" medications and have been shown to work in clinical trials. It is important to note, there is no treatment for RLS which will give a cure. It is only possible to ameliorate the symptoms therefore allowing us to better cope with them.

RLS can be extremely severe in up to twenty percent of sufferers. The symptoms must already be severe and distressing if one is ready to consult a physician or general practitioner (A GP is the UK NHS funded doctor who works with a group of doctors looking after the health and wellbeing of a community, town, or city). When this happens, there are several choices of medications, but some may not be suitable for you personally and any treatment will be closely monitored by your doctor and yourself to ascertain if it is working for you. It may be that several medications are tried before you hit upon one which really suits.

The Medicines and Healthcare products Regulatory Agency (MHRA) has approved the following for RLS in the UK:

- Rotigotine skin patch
- Pramipexole
- Ropinirole

These medications are known as dopamine agonists which work by increasing the levels of dopamine in the blood, which may be very low in sufferers.

Four medications have been approved by the FDA:

- Rotigotine (Neupro)
- Gabapentin Enacarbil (Horizant) – off label.
- Pramipexole (Mirapex)
- Ropinirole (Requip)

Those drugs which may be helpful and are prescribed "off book" are:

- Carbidopa/levodopa (Sinemet and Sinemet CR AKA Parcopa)
- Levodopa
- Clonazepam
- Pregabalin
- Clonidine
- Tramadol (pain relief)
- Lamotrigine

It should be noted that Gabapentin Enacarbil and Pregabalin are now Controlled Drugs since April 2019 under UK law and must be specifically described by a doctor alone to avoid misuse. Off book medications may not necessarily be approved by the FDA.

It would be ill-advised for me to state any dosage of these medications mentioned. This is purely down to your GP or healthcare professional to decide following a full examination of your condition and symptoms.

Medications that increase the dopamine levels in the brain

Each of these medications affects the levels of dopamine secreted by the brain. They include: Pramipexole (Mirapex), Rotigotine (Neupro) and Ropinirole (Requip).

Dopamine is produced in several areas of the brain and is a neurotransmitter allowing transmission of messages within the brain and to other areas. When levels of Dopamine are low, it can be replaced by drugs containing it. Symptoms which may show Dopamine levels are low are muscle cramps, spasms or tremors, aches and pains, and stiffness in the muscles. It is especially important in some neurological diseases such as Parkinson's disease and helps to alleviate symptoms such as tremor. It is easy to see why these types of medications may be prescribed for those of us with RLS. For these medications, short-term side effects include fatigue, light-headedness, and nausea. The long-term or chronic side effects include impulse control disorders, such as daytime sleepiness, and compulsive behaviour such as gambling.

Dopamine agonists and dopamine precursors are medications that mimic the effects of the neurotransmitter dopamine *or* enhance its levels within the body. They act like dopamine by the stimulation of molecules on the surface of certain cells called dopamine receptors (cells that bind with dopamine). In most cases, dopamine agonists such as, Rotigotine patch, Pramipexole, and Ropinirole are recommended as the first line of drug therapy, instead of Levodopa. L-dopa, also known as Levodopa, and is a dopamine precursor that increases the dopamine concentrations in the brain. Because certain enzymes start to immediately break down the available dopamine. Carbidopa, a medication that blocks the activities of such enzymes, is combined with Levodopa. This combined drug is termed Carbidopa/Levodopa.

Most individuals using Levodopa medication may begin to develop severe symptoms of RLS when the dosage wears off. Due to this, the drug is not recommended for long-term use and should be restricted to a dose to be taken twice a week at most.

Drugs affecting calcium channels.

These are drugs which are traditionally used to help lower blood pressure by slowing the movement of calcium into the cells of blood vessel walls and heart. The action widens the vessels and therefore makes it easier for the heart to pump and so our blood pressure lowers.

Drugs which work in this way include the following: Pregabalin (Lyrica), Gabapentin Enarcabil (Horizant), and Gabapentin (Gralise, Neurontin).

These are used as alternative first line therapies for RLS. Gabapentin Enarcabil is an indicant of Gabapentin and has been approved by the FDA for the treatment of RLS as a daily treatment. However effective these drugs may be in the treatment of RLS, they may cause some side effects such as weight gain, depression, a sense of mental fog, unsteadiness, dizziness, and sleepiness.

Benzodiazepines and Opioids

In some cases, the recommended treatment for RLS may include the use of other medications such as, benzodiazepines, sleeping medications and opioids. Certain benzodiazepines such as Temazepam and Clonazepam may be recommended to help enhance sleep.

Opioids are narcotic medications that can help relieve mild to severe symptoms of RLS. Some of these medications are Hydrocodone (Zohydro ER, Hysingla ER), Oxycodone (Roxicodone, Oxycontin, others), Codeine, and Tramadol (Conzip, Ultram).

Opioids would only be prescribed after much deliberation as these are very strong analgesics usually given for very severe pain, and if used in high doses, they become addictive.

Benzodiazepines are soporific drugs which do not so much treat the pain of RLS, but instead help one to relax and allow much needed sleep. It is important to note that they do not completely eliminate the leg sensations. In fact, some of them may cause drowsiness during daytime. They themselves are known to have addictive qualities and therefore are only prescribed for short periods of time, to be used very infrequently when all else fails. Drugs falling into this category include: Temazepam (Restoril), Lorazepam (Ativan), Alprazolam (Xanax), and Diazepam (Valium). In the UK, some of these are controlled drugs and will only be prescribed when absolutely necessary.

Side Effects

To individually describe every drug minutely, to include dosage etc., would be mind-blowingly boring! If you really want to know more in-depth information about the drugs included here, look online, in a copy of the *British National Formulary* (BNF) or even on the information slip in your drug pack. What is more important, is knowing that with every treatment, comes side effects. That is usually the long list of scary stuff on the drug information insert which scares you witless because you may end up having all of them! Be rest assured, that would not generally happen. However, drug companies are, by law, required to disclose every reported side effect for their drugs which is why the list is so scary and of course, you should be aware of what you are potentially going to be putting into your body.

I have broken down the side effects for each drug in the below.

Ropinirole

Common side effects: vomiting and nausea
Very Common side effects: Oedema, dry mouth, gas, raised BP, memory loss, palpitations, tiredness, headache, increased infections, increased muscle movement, stomach pain, indigestion, nervousness and confusion.

Serious side effects: Fainting or loss of consciousness, heart rate changes, low blood pressure, paranoia, agitation, aggressive behaviour, confusion, and hallucinations, high fever, muscle tightness, excessive sleeping, changes in shape, size and colour of the moles on your skin.

Pramipexole

Very common side effects: Dry mouth, nausea, postural hypotension (dizziness while standing), stomach pain, constipation, vomiting, spinning sensation, headache, swellings in the feet and hands, weight or appetite change, blurred vision, dizziness, insomnia, sleep disorders, unusual dreams, amnesia and memory problems, thinking problems or confusion, forgetfulness, impotence, trouble having an orgasm, or loss of interest in sex.

Serious side effects: muscle tenderness or pain, muscle weakness, fainting, hallucinations, light-headedness, sweating, nausea, falling asleep suddenly, extreme drowsiness, uneven or fast heartbeats, cough with pink or white mucus, loss of appetite, rapid weight loss, tremors, uncontrollable movements of your legs, arms, face, tongue, lips, or eyes, twitching, wheezing, dark coloured urine, chest pain, or increased urination.

Rotigotine

Common side effects: trouble staying asleep, trouble falling asleep, sleepiness, headache and nausea and skin irritation (itchiness, swelling and redness).
Serious side effects: dizziness or fainting when standing up, feeling nauseous, sweaty, , elevated heart rate, shortness of breath, light-headedness, severe fluid retention or sudden weight gain, swelling in the ankles or legs, augmentation, worsening severity of RLS symptoms, allergic reactions, change in mental behaviours or health.

Gabapentin Encarbil

Common side effects: dizziness, sedation (a state of induced sleep), somnolence (sleepiness), dizziness while driving, and drowsiness.
Serious side effects: ideation (illusions of a mental image), suicidal behaviours, suicidal thoughts, unusual changes in behaviour or mood and an emergence or worsening of depression.

All the drugs above can also cause serious allergic reactions. It is extremely important that if *any* of the below are experienced and you feel there may be a threat to your life – *dial* 999 (911) *immediately.*

- Difficulty breathing
- Difficulty swallowing
- Swelling of the throat, face, lips, or tongue

The allergic reactions below, although of concern, may not be life threatening and if they persist, medical advice should be sought.

- Hives
- Itchiness
- Skin rash
- Flushing of the skin, redness, deepening of skin colour, temporary warmth
- Swelling under the skin, typically in the feet, hands, or eyelids
- Sulphite sensitivity
- Fever

It is also important you do not stop your medications unless you have been told by a medial practitioner that it's safe to do so. Suddenly stopping some of these medications can cause further unpleasant side effects and need to be weaned off.

Augmentation

Dopamine medications can have a well-known drawback whereupon the effects of the drug become less effective over time and the symptoms of RLS begin to appear earlier in the day. Therefore, relief during the night, is not as effective as before. When this begins to happen, the process is known as Augmentation.

According to Garcia-Borreguero (2016), Augmentation is a consequence of long-term use of dopamine medications, and which can take months or years to develop. Symptoms appear earlier in the day, may spread to other parts of the body, and increase in severity. It tends to be more prevalent when the highest dose of a drug has been used over time (years), and there is no option to increase the dose in line with the severity of the symptoms.

If Augmentation is suspected, then the first option is to split the full dose over the day to try and counter the earlier onset of symptoms. If this does not work, then the next option is to check serum ferritin levels in the blood as iron deficiency anaemia may also have similar symptoms to Augmentation.

Sudden changes in lifestyle may also cause mimicking symptoms. These may be sleep deprivation, recent use of antihistamines or antidepressants, blood loss, decreased mobility and excessive alcohol use. The stopping of opioid treatments may also be a factor. If all else fails, the drug in use should be discontinued and an alternative sought.

Following several clinical trials, it has been shown that all dopamine agonists attribute augmentation, especially when used over a prolonged time. For those using Levodopa, augmentation is most common as it develops in seventy-eight percent of patients. For those on Pramipexole, augmentation is developed at seven percent per year and takes at least nine years for symptoms to show. For Rotigotine users, less augmentation risks have been seen as it is a dopamine agonists transdermal patch.

Reaching augmentation is very frustrating. From personal experience, the pain in one's legs is wretched, pain relief doesn't work well, and many more interrupted nights are a certainty. I had naturally begun to split the dose and found that it is working to counteract the earlier onset of the symptoms. Some time ago I found that by taking a couple of my Pramipexole before going out to a show or the cinema, the discomfort and wanting to move all the time was diminished. At the time I had no idea I was experiencing the early signs of augmentation. I am now well into augmentation and splitting the full dose into three separate doses three times per day. It is working sometimes but even as I write this, I have experienced three wholly sleepless nights this week from the discomfort alone.

Obviously, I will seek the help of my GP to see what the next steps will be, but I do dread being taken off the Pramipexole. I don't know how I will cope with the increase in symptoms. That is why the content of this book is so important to me.

3

THE ROLE OF IRON, VITAMINS, AND MAGNESIUM IN RLS

Let's be honest here. A majority of healthy and fit people, who are not 'fitness freaks' would not have a clue about how much our own bodies rely on a perfect balance of iron, vitamins and minerals. Our body just is. We do not normally consider that for the formation of blood cells, immunity, healing, body tissue, brain and muscle function one must have adequate stores of them. It is only when something makes one feel really bad, out of sorts or sick, one goes looking for answers.

The importance of what is taken into our body cannot be over emphasized when optimising our overall health and, in this case, the improvement of RLS.

Vitamins and minerals, therefore, play essential roles in several body processes, hence, their relevance to overall health. The regular intake of some vitamins and minerals has been linked to the improvement of the condition, and a deficiency in their absorption, a severity.

In this chapter, we will explore the absorption, deficiency, treatment, and benefits of how these vitamins and mineral are associated with RLS.

Iron

Even though the specific cause if RLS is not known, research over the last 20 years has discovered that it is plausible to conclude that those likely to be diagnosed with RLS have an iron deficiency but moreover, the deficiency is significant within the tissues of the brain. The two are different and although a blood test can be used to test the Iron levels within the blood, the single way to test the levels in the brain is by using specialized brain imaging techniques. The tests used in these cases showed that iron was deficient in parts of the brain which were known to make dopamine. When a sample of cerebrospinal fluid was removed via a lumbar puncture, ferritin (the iron storage protein) was shown to be low in these individuals, this was even though their serum levels of ferritin and iron were normal! Thereby proving that diminished brain iron is a significant factor in those with RLS although their serum blood levels may be normal.

Iron is a mineral required by the body to perform many functions and processes playing an essential role in our overall health. In the human body, the haemoglobin of the red blood cells and the myoglobin of the muscle cells house most iron. Iron is also part of many proteins and enzymes.

Treatment and prevention of anaemia, transportation of oxygen and carbon dioxide, promotion of healthy pregnancy and boosting of energy are the most important benefits of iron in the human body.

Iron deficiency anaemia occurs when there are not enough red blood cells carrying vital oxygen from our lungs to our tissues and organs throughout our bodies. Every part of the body requires oxygen in order to function correctly. The less oxygen they receive, the less we function. You may feel weak, fatigued and sometimes, out of breath.

Our bodies need the iron to make more haemoglobin, the protein which carries the red blood cells and therefore oxygen to your organs. Mild anaemia may not be all that noticeable, however the symptoms of a more severe case of iron deficiency anaemia will be more pronounced and severe.

- Shortness of breath
- Headaches
- Light-headedness
- Dizziness
- Irregular and fast heartbeat
- Cold feet and hands
- Chest pain

- Brittle or cracked or spoon-shaped nails
- Pale or yellow skin
- Cracks at the side of your mouth
- Weird cravings of non-foods like coal or dirt
- Hair loss
- Sore and swollen tongue
- Restless legs

Levels of iron in the blood can be affected by many things. For women, the most predominant reasons are menstruation, endometriosis, and pregnancy. Heavy blood loss or an extra call on resources such as during pregnancy cause iron levels to diminish. Other factors may be rectal bleeding, internal bleeding, bowel disease and Peptic ulcer.

There are also factors outside of the body which influences the amount of iron we store in our body. Are we consuming enough iron rich foods for our body to absorb it? We must be reminded that some medications and operations can affect this badly. We absorb iron via our intestines, so what if you have had an operation to remove them? Do you also suffer from Crohn's disease, Coeliac or Ulcerative Colitis which all affect the lower intestine? Do you take drugs to stop acid reflux or anti-inflammatory drugs such as Aspirin or Ibuprofen? Have you had a serious injury causing considerable blood loss?

The point is, there are many reasons why one's iron level may drop. If you notice any of the above symptoms, it may be wise to visit your doctor and have some blood tests carried out to detect any anaemia and commence necessary treatment.

Generally, the treatment for iron deficiency is an iron replacement tablet taken daily for around 6 weeks or until levels increase. However, although they will help one feel more normal, these have side effects worth knowing about. One may become constipated and when you do go, poop is like tar, very black. One may have diarrhoea, nausea, vomiting, stomach discomfort or heartburn leading to a loss of appetite. Again, most people only suffer from one or two of these, don't despair! You will be feeling better and your RLS will have considerably improved.

Therefore, as a patient it is important to rectify low levels of iron in your diet by eating more iron rich sources of food to help manage and control the symptoms of iron deficiency anaemia. In addition, the presence of folate and magnesium in sufficient levels are also shown to be a means through which RLS symptoms can be improved. and are significant to have in one's diet to help build muscles with proper contraction and nerve impulse conduction.

Other ways of increasing the iron in one's body, is to increase those foods which naturally contain more iron. These include:

- Meat
- Seafood
- Leafy green vegetables

- Beans
- Nuts
- Soya
- Fortified grains

It is also known that taking vitamin C with any iron supplements you may take helps the body to absorb the iron.

Vitamin D

Most may associate vitamin D with sunlight, and they would be right. However, there is a little more to it than that. Vitamin D is one of the four fat-soluble vitamins, the others being vitamins E, K and A. It is also an essential vitamin required for normal growth, development, and body function. The two forms of vitamin D are D2, mainly from fortified food and other dairy items and D3, principally from exposure to sunlight and some food items.

Vitamin D is one of the vitamins associated with RLS, and is beneficial in the promotion of strong, healthy bones and teeth, the regulation of calcium and phosphorus levels in the body, the facilitation of the immune system, reduction in risk of type 2 diabetes, and reduced risk of contracting diseases.

Although one does not need a lot of the vitamin, it is one of the vitamins which the human body is incapable of producing by itself. Therefore, we depend on other sources for its production. The main source of vitamin D is exposure to sunlight (ultraviolet exposure). Our body then uses cholesterol to manufacture the vitamin. It is generally advised we should all have at least twenty minutes exposure to the sun without sunscreen to allow us to absorb as much of the rays as we can. Much longer than this is probably not practical or safe, and we should be slapping on the factor 50 after our little bit of sun indulgence. As we in the UK cannot rely on our own weather, the best time to collect those rays is any time the sun is out!

Joking aside, reductions of vitamin D can cause severe rickets and asthma in children and furthermore, according to the National Centre for Biotechnology Information (NCIB), twenty percent and thirty-five percent of adults in the UK and the US respectively are vitamin D deficient.

There are certain risk factors for those persons who may find it difficult to maintain sufficient levels of vitamin D and are:

- Race or having a dark skin
- Age
- Weight
- Chronic diseases such as hyperparathyroidism, kidney and liver disease
- Eating less dairy or fish
- Poor sun exposure due to location
- Use of sunscreens (but very important to safeguard from skin cancers)

- Being inside i.e., chronic illness, kids on game consuls, and computers etc.
- Crohn's disease or celiac disease cannot absorb nutrients including vitamin D.
- Gastric bypass surgery
- Using drugs that impact vitamin D metabolism

The symptoms of having lower than desired levels of vitamin D are as follows:

- Depression
- Lowered immunity
- Impaired wound healing
- Back pain
- Bone pain
- Tiredness
- Fatigue
- Loss of bone density
- Hair loss
- Muscle pains

Vitamin D is present in some of our foods which we should try to consume more of and include:

- egg yolks
- salmon
- mushrooms

- fish
- Vitamin D fortified foods

In recent times, there have been several studies linking vitamin D deficiency to RLS. This connection is not far-fetched since vitamin D is involved in the regulation of calcium and phosphate and the maintenance of healthy and strong bones. A case-controlled study, 'The Association between Vitamin D Level and Restless Legs Syndrome', was conducted at Sleep Medicine and Research Centre, King Abdul-Aziz University Hospital, Saudi Arabia between March, and November 2016. In this study, 201 participants were enrolled, with 78 being RLS positive. One of the tests carried out on the blood samples taken from the participants, was serum 25-hydroxy vitamin D level. The result of the study showed that the association between vitamin D deficiency and RLS remains significant because the risk for development of RLS was significantly higher in vitamin D deficient cases, compared to those who were vitamin D sufficient.

In another study published in August 2014 in the journal 'Sleep and Breathing' titled 'The Effect of Vitamin Supplement on the Severity of Restless Legs Syndrome', where twelve subjects diagnosed with both primary RLS, and vitamin D deficiency also concluded that it may be associated with RLS after treating the patients with vitamin D supplements and noticing a significant improvement in the severity of their symptoms.

The best treatment for vitamin D deficiency is taking vitamin D supplements, although, more exposure to sunlight or inclusion of more vitamin D in your diet may be better advised. A dietary supplement provides nutrients from manufactured products to improve the one's quality of consumption through pills, tablets, capsules, powders, or liquid.

Vitamin B12

Vitamin B12 is an important water-soluble vitamin and is especially vital in the healthy function of the nervous system, formation and maturation of the red blood cells of bone marrow, prevention of anaemia, and DNA synthesis. It also functions as a contributing factor in the metabolism of amino and fatty acids. Like vitamin D, B12 is not produced by the body but is gained through food items, fruits and alternative sources including supplements and injections.

Vitamin B12 is naturally available in:

- meat
- egg
- animal liver and kidney
- Beef
- Tuna
- Trout
- Clam
- Salmon
- Dairy products.

- Nutritional yeast
- Non-dairy milk
- some breakfast cereals.

As with the other Vitamins, the importance of B12 cannot be underestimated. It is quite easy for one to have a deficiency especially if they fall into the following categories: vegetarians or those on a vegan diet, older adults, pregnant or breastfeeding women, those who have had surgery that included their bowels, and those who have conditions that affect their B12 absorption.

Vitamin B12 deficiency can be caused by pernicious anaemia, (the leading cause of B12 deficiency in the UK), immune system disorders, stomach or gut problems, medicines that interfere with B12 absorption, diets and so on.

Signs and symptoms of B12 deficiency.

- Extreme fatigue
- No energy
- Sore tongue
- Mouth ulcers
- Disturbed vision
- Depression
- Confusion
- Muscle weakness
- Memory issues
- Understanding issues

- Problems with judgement
- Pale skin

B12 deficiency can also cause significant damage to the brain which is part of the Central Nervous System and can consequently affect the part of the brain regulating motor functions.

A study was published in the "International Journal of Neurology and Neurosurgery" (July-September 2018) titled "Restless Legs Syndrome as an Early Neurological Manifestation of Vitamin B12 Deficiency". The aims of this study were to measure serum vitamin B12 levels in patients with RLS and assess the response of RLS to its replacement. The study concluded that RLS could be an early neurological manifestation of vitamin B12 deficiency because a significant proportion of RLS patients with low vitamin B12 levels used in the study were promptly relieved of the condition after the administration of vitamin B12 replacement therapy.

Should you think you are suffering from any of the above signs, it is easy enough to ask for a blood test from your doctor to check your levels of B12. If the deficit is severe enough, a treatment of injections may be prescribed. As a patient, you may rather try to increase the levels by taking supplements or consuming vitamin B12 rich foods as the injections once on them, can be a life-long commitment.

Magnesium

Magnesium is the one of the seven essential macro-minerals needed in large amounts in the body. It has over three-hundred cellular functions in the body including nerve and muscle function, regulating blood pressure, and supporting the immune system, making it essential for overall health. It is also involved in many body functions, some of which include bone formation, nervous system regulation, muscle relaxation, calcium regulation and so on. It may also ease constipation and migraine. Magnesium deficiency known as Hypomagnesemia occurs when one is unable to get their required level in the body for several reasons. It can be due to excess consumption of alcohol, gastrointestinal disorders, diabetes, and as a side effect of certain medications.

Studies suggest that about fifty percent of people in the US and Europe get less than the recommended daily amount of magnesium. Magnesium deficiency is also common among African Americans and the elderly and has been linked to health conditions including osteoporosis, type 2 diabetes, high blood pressure, and migraine.

Signs of Magnesium deficiency.

- Muscle twitches and cramps
- Tremors
- Mental health disorders i.e apathy, depression
- Osteoporosis

- Fatigue
- Muscle weakness
- High blood pressure
- Asthma
- Irregular heartbeat including shortness of breath, chest pain and fainting
- Eyelid spasm and flickering

Early research linked RLS to Magnesium deficiency and that Magnesium supplements produced a significant amelioration in the severity of symptoms in RLS. As a result of its Calcium blocking abilities, researchers think if Magnesium level is low, calcium is not blocked which makes nerves become overactive and initiate muscle contraction. Although getting more magnesium is an effective treatment for RLS when it is a co-factor to the condition, it may not be a remedy if there are other factors alongside it.

Generally, magnesium deficiency is corrected by a supplement that will raise levels of the mineral. As stated earlier, research has shown that these supplements can reduce RLS symptoms especially when a deficiency is a co-factor to the condition. Magnesium is also often suggested for RLS based of the anecdotal fact that alongside relieving symptoms of RLS, it is also commonly suggested for leg cramps. As an adult human one contains around 25 mg of magnesium, however, for optimal function far more is required, and it may not always be possible to maintain the required levels. The amount of magnesium needed depends on age, sex and any medical conditions.

If at any time you suspect you may have a low magnesium, it is best to visit your doctor for a blood test to confirm. It may be that a supplement is required to help one raise one's levels. Diet is also factor and foods rich in magnesium should be added or increased in your foods. These include but are not exclusive:

- Flax seed
- Dark leafy vegetables
- Pumpkin seeds, sunflower seeds and chia seeds.
- Almonds, peanuts, cashews and hazelnuts.
- Beans
- Wholegrains
- Dark Chocolate
- Popcorn
- Sunflower
- Cocoa
- Coffee
- Oats
- Milk products

Cereals which have been fortified, magnesium lactate, citrate and aspartate are also dietary supplements.

As you can see, the absence of enough iron, magnesium, vitamin B12 and vitamin D have a significant role in the optimum function of the human body. Any lack of any one of these minerals can significantly affect the symptoms of RLS.

Speaking from a personal standpoint, I know that I struggle if I stop taking any one of my supplements. I was given a borderline result for B12 deficiency some years ago and was given the option to go ahead with the jabs or supplement myself. I opted for the supplements at that point, as I really didn't want to commit to a lifetime of injections (at least until I really need it). However, I don't have a condition which means my levels are so badly low to warrant the jabs, and I am not you. If reading through this chapter, you recognise some of the features of the deficiencies in yourself, I strongly urge you to go to your family doctor and ask for a blood test. It is a good starting point to understanding what you need to do to help yourself.

4

LIFESTYLE AND DIET

DIET

We all know, in our heart of hearts, that we should lead a healthy and productive lifestyle whereupon we eat as we should, exercise as we should and spend equal measure of time in work, play, and sleep. It all sounds very good on paper, but in reality, I ask you to look at yourself and ask the question, 'do I do that?' I'll bet your answer is 'no'. You may try to be fairly active, and watch what you eat, but you have RLS, so sleep is not always an option therefore, it follows that one may not be able to live up to that expectation!

We all need sustenance; food is something most of us enjoy. We live to eat, not eat to live! However, we are learning quickly from research, TV campaigns etc., that we are over-indulging and should pay more heed to what we actually choose to put into our bodies. When you suffer from RLS, this may be more important than we realise at first. The composition of foods, (especially processed foods) can have a real impact on our symptoms. It can both improve and worsen our symptoms. The trick is, to know which does what. We know we should not eat a diet high in carbohydrates if we are diabetic and should watch how much cholesterol containing foods we eat if we have high blood pressure, but what should we be changing about what we eat to help improve our symptoms?

As mentioned above, we can only be helping ourselves if we eat foods rich in iron, magnesium, vitamin B12 and vitamin D. Adding in vitamin C to aid iron absorption is also helpful. But this is not just about what we should be eating, it's also about those substances within foods we should not be eating. These are the chemicals and additives hidden in our foods and which only serve to worsen symptoms. There are even some foods themselves that are not good for RLS. For example, chocolate – I can hear the silent cry of 'Nooooooo' from a lot of you. I was one of those, I lived for the stuff and all its gooey, melting, chocolaty glory. It is not good for us in large amounts. Sorry, but that's it. Moderation is the option or none at all. Foods high in unsaturated fats and sugar, and sugar filled sodas are also not recommended.

All of the above will help us to lose weight, which can only be a good outcome, and should be something any healthy person should aim for. In their 2009, a study 'Obesity and Restless Legs

Syndrome in men and women' Xian Gao et al, discussed the relationship between people being obese and having an increased risk of having RLS. Obesity has been linked to cardio-vascular disease, diabetes and importantly, lower Dopamine receptors and there is your link to RLS.

Caffeine

Caffeine is also a substance which has been known to exacerbate the symptoms of RLS (I can hear more cries of despair). It has been shown that reducing or removing caffeine from the diet of RLS sufferers, can help to calm restlessness, and in mild cases of RLS, it can improve symptoms and aid better sleep. Caffeine stimulates the nerve cells of the brain, but it is not addictive and is considered a safe ingredient in our food items. If you have a lot of it, you may feel dependent on it. In moderation, the feeling of dependence is not likely to arise, but this means only two to three reasonable cup size beverages per day! If your consumption is more, maybe you should really consider cutting down.

It is also interesting to note that breastfeeding mothers can pass on caffeine to their infants through breast milk. If your child has difficulty sleeping, is irritable and won't settle, consider what your intake of caffeine is. Is it too high, 'cos your baby is wired!

Caffeine will also take around five to six hours to clear your system after drinking a single cup of coffee. Therefore, it is usually advised not to drink it in the afternoon especially if you have difficulty sleeping anyway.

Age is also a factor in the metabolism of caffeine, the older you are, the longer it takes for your body to pass it from your system. If you choose to reduce your intake of caffeine or cut it out entirely, you may get the following symptoms: fatigue, difficulty concentrating, muscle pain, nausea, and headache. It would be tempting to take pain relief to help this, but beware, caffeine is also added to certain over-the-counter analgesics (pain relief) one would usually take for headache. It helps the body to absorb the drug and helps to prevent the likely hood of addiction.

Check what you are drinking and eating if you are cutting down on caffeine, the following contain it at various concentrations.

- Tea
- Coffee
- Chocolate
- Certain over the counter medicines
- Coca Cola /Pepsi/Monster/ Energy drinks and other sodas.

Switch to alternative drinks and foods. Below is a list but it is not exclusive, there will be too many to mention.

- Green tea, herbal tea – Tea Pigs, Twining, shops own brand
- Decaffeinated tea – Clipper, Twining's, Tetley
- Decaffeinated coffee – shops own, Kenco, Nescafe
- Shops own brand colas and fizzy drinks
- Roasted chicory drink
- Jamun seed kernel coffee.
- Pure Heavenly

Ok, I am a bit biased with the Pure Heavenly chocolate. It is delicious and gluten free, dairy free, vegan friendly, and low sugar! There are other brands available to such as Moo Free Chocolates and Hotel Chocolate amongst others.

Gluten

Although there is no scientific evidence that gluten causes RLS, there has been research to see whether avoiding gluten eases RLS. Gluten is a protein found in Wheat, Barley, and even Rye. It can also be found in baked foods and treats like breads as well as in some condiments, soups, and even salad dressings. It is safe to say that gluten is found in all flour used to make pastries and can also appear in most foods, so you must check out every food that you make or purchase to reduce your gluten intake.

I wondered whether I may be gluten intolerant as after eating the foods above, I became uncomfortably bloated and full of wind. Whilst browsing Facebook one day, I found one of those offers where you send off some of your hair and receive back a report of all the intolerances one may have. When my report arrived back, I was very shocked to see just how much I had sensitivity to milk, gluten, dairy, *chocolate*, cheese, coconut, cauliflower(!), E numbers etc. It made interesting reading. Needless to say, I have made changes and at the time of writing, I think they have made a difference in my general wellbeing, but I am yet to see whether my RLS is affected positively or not.

Alcohol

I must discuss alcohol. It cannot be avoided. We all know it is fun to drink in moderation, it tastes nice, makes us feel good and can enable us to do things we may not have had the courage to do before (ask someone to marry, ask someone out, tell a parent something difficult). Big but here, it can also be amazingly destructive to us. Over-indulgence leads to dependency and in the long run can cause other health conditions such as:

- Cirrhosis of the liver
- Damage to brain cells
- Cancers of the Gastro-Intestinal tract
- Depression
- Dementia
- Pancreatitis

- Worsening symptoms of RLS
- Disrupted sleep patterns.

Once again, speaking from experience, I know for myself drinking alcohol is a big *NO*. It definitely has an effect on my legs, and I find that they hurt more for longer. Medication doesn't work as well, and I invariably end up awake and pacing the house all night. If I want to drink, I choose something I know will not affect it. That seems to be Gin for me, but if I drink any sort of wine... I find it interesting to note that the sensitivity test I had done showed I can't drink any variety of wine, but I am not sensitive to Gin. Consequently, I don't drink much at all now, two glasses are about my limit, and they need to be really small ones. What do you feel when you drink any alcohol? Are your symptoms worse when you drink something specific?

The recommended intake of alcohol in the UK is: Men and Women – 14 units of alcohol per week (NHS). In the USA it's two drinks a day for men and one or less for women (CDC).

To summarise, eating a balanced diet that is rich in microminerals, has reduced fats and sugars and without alcohol and caffeine, will help to lessen the seriousness of the symptoms you experience.

It is important to stay as healthy as possible by practicing common-sense diet dos and don'ts.

- Eat different fruits and vegetables especially dark leafy greens.
- Unless you are a vegetarian, cultivate the habit of eating a variety of Iron-rich lean meats.
- Eat legumes, tree nuts and seeds.
- Avoid eating lots of processed foods.
- Avoid foods and beverages high in sugar or high-fructose corn syrup.
- Avoid fried foods and other foods that can make you gain weight.

Change of Lifestyle

Although we wish it were possible, there is currently no known cure for RLS, but if you have this disorder, a few things can help you improve the quality of your life. A change of lifestyle is one of them. We have discussed diet including foods and drinks, good and bad, for us above. This section talks about the rest.

As you might have noticed earlier, the end goal of every RLS treatment is to correct underlying habits or conditions that worsen or trigger the symptoms, improve the quality of one's sleep, and to relieve or prevent symptoms of RLS. If you suffer from mild RLS, then changes to the style of your life might just be all the treatment that you need.

Making the Changes: Medication

One of the most important things to consider is that RLS is usually accompanied by a chronic condition of some sort. Along with these conditions comes a whole arsenal of drugs we depend on to keep pain at bay or keep us functioning in body and mind.

Unfortunately, as discussed earlier, medication can have side effects of their own, some of which may actually be augmenting the effects of RLS or in some cases, may be the cause. It is worth checking out the information leaflets in the boxes and trawl through the section regarding this and if you do spot one which may worsen the condition, it may be a good idea at this time to consult with your doctor to see whether your medication can be changed to an alternative or removed completely. You must *never* take the initiative to stop taking drugs yourself, it could be a dangerous move because they are likely to be very necessary for your other condition(s). Some also require a weening off period to avoid unpleasant side effects just stopping them may cause.

Drugs which may affect your RLS include, but are not exclusive:

- Antihistamine drugs_such as Diphenhydramine (Benadryl).
- Antipsychotic drugs such as Olanzapine (Zyprexa) or Haloperidol (Haldol).
- Lithium (Lithobid)

- Tramadol (Ultram)
- Levothyroxine (Levoxyl)
- Tricyclic antidepressants such as Amoxapine (Asendin) or Amitriptyline (Elavil).
- Selective serotonin reuptake inhibitors (SSRIs) such as Escitalopram (Lexapro), Sertraline (Zoloft), or Fluoxetine (Prozac).
- Anti-nausea drugs Prochlorperazine (Compro) or Metoclopramide (Reglan)

As you may have noticed, there are some over-the-counter medications which can also give rise to RLS. It's important that you check with the pharmacist before purchasing some cold and flu remedies, antihistamines, and anti-sickness drugs. It may be beneficial to ask the doctor to prescribe something which will not set of your symptoms rather than chance buying them yourself.

Exercise

If you have RLS, exercises can help you feel better. According to the National Institutes of Health, moderate exercises may help ease the symptoms of mild RLS. Aerobic exercises and lower body resistance training done three times per week for a duration of twelve weeks has been shown to drastically reduce the symptoms. However, a common misconception when someone states a change in lifestyle is required, is that one must make huge changes to our diet, exercise, habits and sleep – and do it all at once. This is *not* the case. The point is that you start to make *small* changes as often as you can so that those changes don't have so much of an impact on your life and are barely noticeable. It may be that you start by changing from sugar to a sweetener, or to caffeine-free tea and coffee and leaving a stretch of time between each change. This helps you to adapt slowly and integrate those changes causing you minimal upset and allowing you to adjust. It is the same with trying to change those aspects of our lives which a lot of us do not want to tackle – fitness.

You must have some idea of what you may be capable of in regard to taking up some form of exercise. Again, there are misconceptions that we should be dashing out of our front doors wearing head to toe Lycra, sweat bands and an Apple watch and doing 10 laps of the neighbourhood. Seeing me in said costume is likely to imprint an image onto your brain you are not going to forget in a hurry! Besides, most of us can just about think about taking a short walk due to other chronic conditions.

Do what you can, as often as you can, for as long as you can. With perseverance you will improve. The NHS website has some useful tips regarding what low, moderate and vigorous activity are. It also talks about duration and frequency of exercise and considers the low impact exercises suitable for those who are differently abled.

If you have a dog and walk it regularly, try to extend the time you are out. Perhaps pick up the pace a little and walk more briskly, just enough to make you slightly more out of breath and raise your pulse rate. Maintain it for a short period and then drop back to your normal pace. When you have settled down from the exertion, do it again! Your stamina will gradually get better. Even if you don't own a dog, borrow one or grab a friend for short walks around your neighbourhood, again gradually building on the time you are out and the length of the walk. Do not forget about the nature walks around your locality, it is all good for variety. There may be a local rambling or walking club in your town who hold weekly walks. It is a great way to make friends too. Besides, think of all that wonderful vitamin D you will be soaking up!

If all you can do is walk gingerly around the ground floor of your house, do it a couple of times more and then rest. Do not sit in your chair for so long, get up and stretch and move. Your joints will thank you for it and your brain will too for giving it a break from your computer or work. You should ideally move at least once an hour to help relieve your joints and muscles. Giving your brain a break also enables you to return to what you were doing with clearer thoughts. Even climbing the stairs is exercise, do it a few times a day. Do not take the lift if you can walk up or down the stairs – it all helps.

Swimming.

Swimming is one of the best exercises to help keep you fit. It is low impact, keeping the stress to your body at a minimum, ideal if you have other bony or muscular issues. It builds on muscle strength, cardio fitness, and endurance, helps you tone your muscles, helps to maintain a healthy weight, and helps to maintain health heart and lungs. There are also other benefits:

- It improves posture, your coordination and balance
- Improves your flexibility
- It is relaxing
- Peaceful
- Available in many places
- It is a fun social act

It is always a good idea to check with your local swimming pool or club to see what they offer. Many pools offer lane swimming either first thing in the morning or later at night before they close. They have lanes of various speeds, so if you are a slow swimmer, you do not need to worry about others whizzing past you. They also offer swimming lessons for adults and aqua aerobics which is a lot of fun and builds on your fitness.

Cycling

Cycling can help calm your symptoms, especially when it is done at a moderate pace of ten miles per hour or slower. It may be worth dragging out your old bike, grabbing one to do up from Freecycle or Facebay, and bringing back some of those childhood memories. Cycling has become a little safer in the UK since the advent of cycleways and in the USA the popularity of biking had risen from 43 million to 47.5 million in the space of three years to 2017. It is a good lone pastime or a social one if you invite family and friends along or join a local club. Be safe, and make sure you use helmets, lights, and dayglow safety clothing. As per usual, take it easy, start off slowly.

I have tried cycling myself. I bought a second-hand bike from a friend. It was purple, (my favourite colour) and in really good nick. I pumped up the tyres, replaced the brake pads and was good to go. Now, bearing in mind, I had not actually been on a bike for over twenty years, I was very impressed that I had remembered how to even stay upright on one, let alone pedal and steer as well. Being particularly chuffed with myself, I decided to do a roughly two-and-a-half-mile block around the roads in my area. It was a beautiful day, sun was shining, birds were singing, and I had a lovely ride and didn't manage to get myself killed. Achievement! The following day, I was ready to do it all again, but when I tried to get out of bed, I had a nasty shock! The seat I had ridden on the day before, had not been all that comfortable, but having an ample bum, I thought nothing of it. Perhaps I should have, because my ass was so sore, I could barely stand upright, let alone walk! My pelvic bones and lady parts were so bruised and painful and stayed that way for a good few days. All I could do was hobble; I was in so much pain! Needless to say, the bike got passed on to some other poor mug and I haven't ridden one since. Cycling is not for me! The moral of this story is, don't rush in to biking if you haven't been on one for years. Make sure your seat is padded and very comfortable and meant for your gender. Then take it easy and start slow. Believe me, it's no fun having a bruised fanny!

The Gym

There will almost certainly be a gym near to you. It may be part of a pool complex, or a stand-alone in the converted warehouse on the industrial estate, but there will be a lot of them nearby. It is a growing trend. Whether you love or hate them, they are a great way to begin to get fit under instruction from the attendants. On application you will be asked to carry out a fitness test, usually including a check on your heart rate, BP and asking what you want from the sessions. On your first visit, you will be taken through the equipment and given an explanation of what it will do for you. They will start you off gently and monitor your progress until you are happy to go it alone. The idea is not to try to compete with the Olympic running star on the treadmill next to you, it's just to do what you can and feel happy about doing it. No need for embarrassment either. If you look around you while you are working out, most will have headphones in and won't be worrying about what you are doing or your size. Everyone joins for their own reasons.

Personally, I view the gym with trepidation. I have belonged to a gym before, but although I was doing OK and sort of enjoyed it, I failed on the commitment aspect. It didn't help that I was actually quite unwell requiring an operation. I didn't go back after that. It should not be the same for you. If you feel you can go to the gym several days a week, go for it, but don't forget not to tire yourself, especially if you have an underlying chronic condition such as chronic fatigue syndrome or fibromyalgia.

Exercising at Home

Of course, you can make your own gym at home. You can use tins of soup as weights, the stairs as a 'step', the back of chairs as a balance for your stretches. It is surprising what you can come up with! Use the internet for inspiration and the nice thing is it costs nothing.

I have found a particularly good exercise video for restless legs stretches on retches on YouTube from Ask Doctor Jo. She is also very good at other exercises to help musculoskeletal issues. Here are some other gentle stretches which may be of benefit to us.

Calf Stretch.

1. Stretch out your arms with your palms flat against the wall and your elbows slightly apart.
2. Bend your right knee slightly and move your left leg back a foot or two with the foot and the heel flat on the floor.
3. Hold this position for twenty to thirty seconds.

4. Next, bend the left knee while keeping the foot and heel flat on the floor.
5. Switch your legs and repeat the process.

Hip Flexor Stretch.

1. Place a chair with its back against the wall and stand facing the chair.
2. Raise your left foot and rest it flat on the chair. Ensure that your knees are bent.
3. Keep your spine as neutral as you can and press your pelvis forward until you feel the top of your right thigh at a stretch.
4. Hold this position for twenty to thirty seconds.
5. Switch your legs and repeat the process.

Front Thigh Stretch.

1. Stand parallel to a wall for balance.
2. Pull out one of your ankles to the rear with the other leg still straight.
3. Hold this position for twenty to thirty seconds.
4. Switch your legs and repeat the process.

Yoga

Yoga stretches and poses can be extremely helpful to relieve the symptoms of RLS. It can help you feel less stressed and help you sleep better. The exercises are designed to be simple and teach your body and core strength. Give the below a try to help you find relief.

Vipariti Karani

Vipariti karani is known as 'the legs up the wall pose' and is effective, especially if you stand or sit all day.

1. Lie on your back and extend your legs up at a 90-degree angle against the wall.
2. Stay in this position for five to twenty minutes to ease symptoms.
3. However, if you are on your period, are pregnant, have diabetes or uncontrolled high blood pressure, you should not carry out this pose.

Paschimottonasana

Paschimottonasana is also known as 'the seated forward fold'.

1. Sit with your feet straight extended in front of you.
2. Lengthen your spine.
3. Fold yourself forward from the hips.
4. Grasp both of your feet with your hands.
5. Breathe deeply and calmly and hold the position for five to ten breaths.

Setu bandhanasana

Setu bandhanasana is also known as 'the supported bridge pose'. It is usually carried out in the morning or in the night and when you feel tensed or wound up and you want to get some kinks out.

1. Lie on your back with your knees bent and your feet flat on the floor with the hips distantly apart.
2. Support your lower back with a yoga block or a firm pillow.
3. Let your body relax.
4. Stay in this position for two to five minutes.
5. Remove the block or pillow and breathe in and out five more times.
6. Roll to one side.
7. Push yourself into a seated position with your hands.

I have also found quite a good YouTube channel called Ventuno Yoga which specifically gives 8 yoga stretches to help calm RLS. I have not tried Yoga before, I am sure it's harder than it looks, so just take your time, and build up to doing more reps of the poses or the length of time spent in the pose.

Giving up Smoking

To give up smoking for some will seem like an impossible task. But to allow yourself to feel improvement of the symptoms of RLS, one should really make a firm effort to at least try to give up. Remember what I said at the beginning of the chapter about making small but significant changes slowly over a period of time? This is one of those changes you can do either way, go 'cold turkey' or take your time and gradually cut down before stopping.

Society in the UK has been steered away from this antisocial behaviour by UK laws passed which prevent us from smoking in pubs and indoor areas. We are not meant to smoke in company vehicles either, so we have been pushed outdoors to enjoy a cigarette. Even the use of Vapes is frowned upon indoors and it is becoming apparent, they are no good for your health either. To breach these laws incurs heavy fines. The cigarette packs have been adorned with alarming pictures of patients suffering from diseases caused by smoking, there is no advertising as there was in the 1970's and cigarettes are hidden away behind shutters in shops.

US law was changed as recently as July 2018 to ban smoking in enclosed spaces in many states but there are a lot of exemptions depending on whether the state has cigar clubs, Casinos etc., and some allow hotels to designate smoking areas.

The message is clear, it is not good for you, you should give it up. It can lead to breathing difficulties, oral, pancreatic, and oesophageal cancers; it stains fingers and the furniture in our homes, makes clothing and homes smell of stale smoke, but it is also addictive making giving up one of the hardest things a smoker can be asked to do.

I am not a smoker, (OK, I smoked for about 6mths when I needed a break from my really trying 2½ year old. It was smoke or kill the kid. Smoking was preferable). Neither am I going to bang on about how bad it is, I have already said that.

In their study, 'Cigarette smoking as a risk factor or an exacerbating factor for restless legs syndrome and sleep bruxism, 2009', G.L Lavigne et al. carried out a study on 2019 Canadians who smoked, had RLS or ground their teeth. At the end, they concluded that the presence of smoking had no effect on RLS symptoms or sleep. So, it would appear nicotine does not have an impact

Giving up is entirely your choice but it may be worth knowing that it can only be beneficial to do so. The timeline below demonstrates this.

Time post giving up	Benefit
1 hour	Blood pressure begins to lower, and circulation improves.
12 hours	The body starts to cleanse itself of excess carbon monoxide returning body levels of oxygen to normal.
1 day	The risk of heart attack starts to decrease as does the risk of stroke.
2 days	Sense of smell and taste begins to return as damaged nerve endings begin to heal.
3 days	The body has depleted levels of nicotine, which causes withdrawal. Around this time the worst cravings for cigarettes can be experienced along with headaches and and changes in mood.
1 month	Lung function is improving as damage to the lining is healed and lung capacity improves. There may be less shortness of breath and coughing and an improved ability to do cardiovascular exercises.
1-3 months	Circulation improving all the time.
9 months	Lungs are well on the way to healing, cilia have regrown helping to prevent a build-up of mucus and lung infections.
After 1 year	The risk of coronary heart disease has decreased by 50% and continues to drop.
After 5 years	The body has healed enough for blood vessels and arteries to have returned to near normal size helping to prevent the likelihood of blood clots. This lowers the risk of stroke which will continue to improve as time goes on. changes in mood.
After 10 years	The chance of developing a lung cancer and dying from it are halved compared to someone still smoking. The chances of mouth, throat and pancreatic cancers have also reduced significantly.
After 15 years	The risk of developing coronary heart disease or pancreatic cancer has reduced to the same as someone who has never smoked.
After 20 years	The risk of death from lung disease, pancreatic and lung cancer drops to the same level as that of a person who has never smoked.

Medical News Today Nov 19, 2018

Healthy Sleep Habits

As this subject has a whole chapter to itself, I won't discuss healthy sleep habits here. Please see Chapter 5.

We have discussed in this chapter how small changes lead to bigger changes regarding diet and lifestyle habits. I know that for me, personally, changing any of my habits has taken a very long time to get around to, let alone actually achieve. It is only recently since I have had my sensitivity test carried out, spiralling out of control blood sugars, constantly high blood pressure, and weight issues, that I had that epiphany moment and finally realised I was doing myself a disservice. I have looked into my drugs, and I am trying to come off Sertraline after around twenty years (it's one of those which makes RLS worse), have eliminated all those foods (well most) from my diet to which I have a sensitivity and my diabetic nurse has put me onto a new jab which helps regulate blood sugar levels but has a side effect of helping you to lose weight too! Hopefully, after all this, I may lose enough weight to fall out of type II diabetes and improve the RLS symptoms. Everything is being done over time and is manageable to me.

The implications of improving diet and lifestyle are far reaching and can only benefit us as individuals in the long run. We know there is no cure for RLS, and we can only mitigate the symptoms, but this will not happen unless you try to change, and you will be even more healthy generally for it.

5

TO SLEEP, PERCHANCE, TO DREAM!

The need for sleep can never be underestimated. A lack of sleep can do so much harm to us, both physically and mentally. As a healthy adult, we should expect to have between seven- and nine-hours uninterrupted sleep per night. I will let you sit back and absorb that for a moment. Between seven and nine hours! You can stop the manic laughing now, that's the guidance advised by the SleepFoundation.org. According to their chart, teens need a bit more, up to ten hours and older people over sixty-five need a little less, between seven and eight hours. I bet you can't remember the last time you actually managed to get in those hours. In most households, it's not happening if you have young children, are a carer for an older adult or child, have needy pets, a career where you keep long hours, have a chronic health condition, or have RLS. Of course, you may have all the above and consider it a luxury to even get a couple of hours in consecutive blocks. Therefore, most of us are sleep deprived to some degree, stress plays a large part in it particularly for the time during the 2020 Covid pandemic. To have RLS on top, takes the biscuit. This is after all, why you picked this book!

The lack of sleep affects both mental and physical health, therefore, when you don't sleep properly, it can have a serious effect on your energy during the day, productivity, emotional balance, decision making, overall health and even what you weigh. We need to understand what it means to sleep well and to be sleep deprived.

When we sleep, our body goes through a sleep cycle which looks something like this:

Stage 1 – Drowsy – first 5 – 10 minutes.
Stage 2 – Light Sleep – lasts for 20 minutes.
Stage 3 – Moderate Sleep.
Stage 4 – Deep Sleep – lasts 30 minutes.
Stage 5 – REM – Rapid Eye Movement.

We do not pass through these stages in only one pass, but rather the cycle continues through the night, ending in Stage 5 REM and then starting again with Stage 1. As an adult one would spend around fifty percent in stage 2 sleep and about twenty percent in REM sleep.

Sleep Deprivation.

> sleep-deprived
> *adjective* - suffering from a lack of sleep. (*Oxford English Dictionary (OED)*)

The phenomena of sleep deprivation are common in our modern society. We all have pressures which give us sleepless nights and for some, this can be a real concern. Studies have shown that even one night of deprivation can have considerable effects on how we function. Almost everything can be affected from our level of tiredness, emotions, thinking, alertness, and other cognitive processes. In his study *'Effects of sleep deprivation on cognition'* in 2010, William D.S. Killgore discussed that we are not all the same and our reaction to sleep deprivation will be different to someone else's. However, there is evidence that deprivation causes a significant reduction of the tolerance of pain for individuals which included physical discomfort, headache, body pain, stomach, and muscle pain. Individuals may also report low mood, increased irritability, and labile emotions. Memory can be significantly affected as sleep is critical to these processes.

There are two types of insomnia: Primary insomnia – the inability to sleep is not associated with any other health condition. Causes of primary insomnia include life stresses, noise, light, temperature, changes in daily life, or bad habits. It is usually transient and will go away with the help of sleeping tablets and changes to routines.

Secondary insomnia – is associated with another health issue. Causes of secondary insomnia may include mental health issues, medications, pain or discomfort at night, alcohol, caffeine, tobacco, endocrine problems and of course, sleep disorders – sleep apnoea or RLS. This needs more attention and treatment unlike the acute insomnia and a trip to a medical practitioner is best in this case.

Since the desire to move one's legs are key with RLS, staying asleep becomes difficult for lots of patients suffering from it. According to research, eighty-eight percent of people with RLS reported at least one sleep related symptom. RLS symptoms often take effect a few minutes after laying down at night; rather than sleeping, individuals with this syndrome will kick, squirm, or massage their legs to reduce the displaying sensations. This is the reason why some are even forced to get out of bed for a walk, to pace around, or even do some stretches to relieve themselves of these sensations. The inability to sleep properly causes other things associated with anxiety, heart diseases, obesity, and depression; all these RLS patients are at greater risk from. At a recent wedding, I was talking to one lady who became very interested when I mentioned I was writing this book. She told me her legs were really active at night, they jumped continually and were so painful she tried to avert her mind over to the pain of her jamming her leg between the bed and the wall just to try to feel something different. I was shocked to hear this to say the least. I also came across another man who stated he had similar issues with his legs at night. I hope when they read this volume, there is something within the pages which helps them on their RLS journey.

Returning to the fact that even one night without sleep can have significant impact of how our body functions, Donga *et al* (2010) showed that insulin resistance and glucose intolerance was affected. Therefore, this would have a significant impact on those individuals who were type 2 diabetics.

Furthermore, E.M. Brady *et al* (2018) discovered that there was:

> *'..an interrelationship between sleep, metabolic disfunction and obesity.'* The study went on to say, *'Sleep is a health behaviour that is more often over-looked or dismissed ...To recognise, prioritise and respond to your natural requirements for sleep above social demands has the potential to improve health and well-being'.*

They further go on to say that to introduce sleep hygiene measures is a relatively low- cost way to help prevent certain chronic disease.

Finally, to bring the research right up to date, Jane Falkingham *et al* (2020) studied sleep deprivation during the first lock down of the Covid 19 pandemic. They were looking at how it may affect the mental and physical condition of their subjects. These subjects were women with young children and Black, Asian, and Minority Ethnic (BAME) individuals. They concluded that stress levels had risen during this time due to worries regarding, finances, health, change in social interaction and daily routine, and *all* of this affected sleep. Women appeared to be more affected by sleep deprivation than men were and those from the BAME backgrounds were affected more deeply likely due to their susceptibility to the Covid infection. Home working and home schooling contributed to disrupted sleep leading to physical and mental health changes. This is all very interesting, but what about RLS?

When sleep is disturbed by your leg movements, then it would be reasonable to assume RLS. Some of the signs of sleep related issues associated with the RLS are difficulties in initiating sleep, less recuperative sleep, tiredness, or taking more naps in the day than the average person. One needs to prepare beforehand by taking prescribed medications, analgesics, or holistic pain relief, or inevitably it prevents those of us with RLS from sleeping properly at night. I will bet being woken in this manner is something you can relate to.

Despite all the discomfort we suffer, it is possible to get a good night's sleep and feel as good as new the following day, but it can come at a price. One will need to watch what one does during the day which may impact on being able to have a restful night. Below are some tips for better sleep.

Tips for Sleep

1. **Be in harmony with your body's natural sleep-wake cycle.** One of the most important methods that can help you sleep well is to keep in sync. with your body's natural sleep-wake cycle or what is being referred to as the circadian rhythm. This emphasizes that keeping the same sleeping and waking schedule will do more good than harm, keeping your body refreshed and energized in the morning. This is very much more effective than sleeping the same number of hours at the different times, even if altered for just an hour or two.
2. **Endeavor to sleep and wake at the same time daily.** When you continually practice this, it helps to set your internal clock which keeps you posted about when to sleep, as well as when to wake. The way to do this is to pick the time you normally feel quite tired and worn out during the day, so that you don't end up tossing and turning through the night. There should not be a need for an alarm if your body gets used to a routine for sleeping but should you occasionally need an alarm to wake you, it is advisable to think about an earlier bedtime.
3. **Avoid sleeping in.** The purpose of maintaining a strict and disciplined sleep cycle is to create a pattern for yourself which your body becomes used to

ensuring you to always sleep well. Therefore, it is not good to sleep in during the weekends because this ends up disrupting the perfectly scheduled sleep routine you are mentally attuned to. Create activities for yourself even during the weekends that will require you to maintain the same sleep pattern, or you can opt for a short nap during the day to balance things up. Don't make up for lack of sleep by sleeping in, it disrupts the carefully laid foundation you have laid for your sleep pattern.

4. **Nap smartly**. Although napping during the day is a way to make up for the lost sleep you might have experienced, it can pose a threat to your carefully laid sleep schedule. Napping during the day can even make things worse if not done properly. So, do not over nap! You can limit your naps to about fifteen to twenty minutes in the early afternoon because any time after that may disrupt your sleep cycle.
5. **War against post dinner drowsiness**. If you become sleepy right before your bedtime, you can engage in some stimulating, fun activities that will prevent you from going straight to bed. Get up from where you are and do something to keep you occupied until your fixed bedtime. Succumbing to drowsiness means that you may wake up during the night and find it difficult to drop back off to sleep.
6. **Consider taking a melatonin supplement**. The

tablet is often used when treating insomnia and may improve sleep quality and one's energy for the next day. However, it has now been recognised that to use melatonin may diminish dopamine levels and can thus exacerbate restless legs. It may not be 'recommended', but many sleep doctors do use it.

Influence your exposure to light.

1. **Keep your exposure to light under control.** Melatonin is a hormone that occurs naturally and is controlled by light exposure which helps regulate your sleep-wake cycle. The brain secretes more melatonin when it is dark which makes you sleepy and secretes less in lightened places that makes you more alert. However, today, there are lots of artificial factors that can alter your body's production of melatonin and move the circadian rhythm.
2. **Let yourself be exposed to bright sunlight in the morning.** Make this time very much closer to the time you get up and are having your first cup of tea or coffee for the day. You can eat breakfast by a sunny window or al fresco outside with the light on your face. This will wake you up, as well as leave you feeling refreshed.
3. **Find things to do outside during the day.** Spend your work breaks or any free time you have

during the day in the sunlight. You can take a walk alone or with the dog, exercise, or do some gardening or outside DIY; walk your dog again later during the day rather than later at night. Don't underestimate the effects of UV rays on your health.

4. **Enjoy the sunlight.** Find a way to direct some natural light into your house or workspace. During the day, keep your curtains and blinds open so that you can bathe in the sunlight.
5. **Light therapy box.** If or when necessary, you can make use of a light therapy box. This replicates sunlight especially during the cold winter days. It helps you maintain the needed and necessary dose if daily sunlight required for proper sleep. It also helps to alleviate the effects of seasonal affective disorder (SAD).
6. **Avoid bright electrical screens.** In the preceding hour to two of your bedtime, it is best to do away with bright screens. The blue light reflected by electronic gadgets like your phone, computer, tablet, or television, can be quite disturbing. Therefore, you can do well to reduce the impact of this by making use of smaller screened device, reduce the brightness totally, or use light-altering apps like f.lux (available online) among others.
7. **Avoid late-night television.** It is good to discipline yourself and be able to say no to late-night

TV. The light from the television pushes down melatonin, and often, the programs are mainly stimulating rather than being relaxing. Therefore, you can try other methods to help you fall asleep such as reading books, listening to music or to audio books. Whatever works for you, as long as you avoid bright screens.

8. **Avoid reading with backlit devices.** Making use of your phone or tablet to read books before going to sleep is not avoiding bright screens! It flies in the face of the above advice. This is because the backlight of these devices is far more distracting than e-readers that have no light source of their own.
9. **Darken the room before sleeping**. This is just common sense and where your curtains, shades, or blinds come in to play. Close window coverings shutting out light and reflections. You can also make use of a sleep mask to cover your eyes and reduce as much light as possible. Also consider turning off light emitting devices.
10. **Keep internal house lights down.** Instal a night light or get a flashlight handy in case it is necessitated to move in the night. Rather than being in the room, you can place this dim light on the landing. The lack of a brighter light will help you to fall back to sleep more easily.
11. **Exercise During the Day.** Exercising regularly will

help you sleep better at night and more alert during the day. According to research, regular exercise also improves the symptoms of insomnia and sleep apnoea. It can also determine how much deep restorative sleep you get during the night. The more you exercise consistently, the more you benefit from it sleep wise. Even something as little as a ten-minute walk will help improve your sleep quality beyond your expectations. As discussed previously, you don't need to rush the process but be gradual about it all. Be patient and concentrate on developing an exercise habit which improves over time. It is important to note that exercise also boosts your metabolism, raises body temperature, and stimulates hormones such as cortisol. Exercising in the morning or afternoon is no problem at all and should be encouraged. However, exercising too close going to bed may cause disruption in your sleep pattern and may be too stimulating. All forms of exercise, be it moderate or a vigorous, should be done and over with at least three hours before you retire to sleep. Relaxing and low impact exercises like yoga, or light stretching in the evening can help promote sleep.

12. **Watch what you eat and drink**. Eating too late in the day can influence your sleep pattern. All that matters is that you know your body, become friends with it, and do what will bring peace and good health to it. While a night snack before going to bed may help

some sleep well through the night, others may have indigestion or difficultly dropping off to sleep. If you are someone who likes a supper try a banana, milk or yogurt, half a turkey sandwich, a little bowl of whole grain or low sugar cereal. These will help your body to maintain a balanced blood sugar over night. This is important because low blood sugar is a trigger for RLS, which is thereby kept in balance by foods that contain protein.

13. **Reduce caffeine and nicotine.** After drinking, caffeine can cause ten to twelve hours of sleep dysfunction before wearing off. Likewise, smoking is another stimulant that can disturb your sleep. Therefore, it's advised these are avoided closer to sleeping.
14. **Do not take big meals in the late evening**. Endeavor to fix your dinnertime for earlier in the evening. Avoid foods that are too rich, spicy, or acidic. Eating these kinds of food during the day is not a bad thing but eating them about two hours before your bedtime is what might really cause trouble for your sleep-wake cycle not to mention, your digestion.
15. **Avoid sugary foods and refined carbs.** When you consume sugar and refined foods during the day such as white rice, white bread, or pasta, these foods can trigger wakefulness during the night due to

bloating and a raise in energy levels and raise the blood sugar.

16. **Do not drink too much fluid in the evening**. Drinking water is very important because it helps replenish cells and keep us properly hydrated. Some teas such as Chamomile may be beneficial because it doesn't have caffeine as an additive. Another drink which may help to produce melatonin (sleep hormone) production in the brain is a tart cherry juice. However, drinking too much of anything in the evening is not a great idea. While it does not have an adverse effect on your body, it will keep you taking trips to the bathroom all through the night when you should be sleeping.

Learn methods to get back to sleep

It is absolutely normal to wake up at some point during the night, but you must learn to go back to sleep almost immediately. However, if you have trouble going back to sleep, you may try the following ways:

1. **Do not stress!** Do not panic or be concerned about your inability to go back to sleep. Try to stay 'out' of your head because it will keep your mind too busy with thoughts and will serve only keep you awake for longer. Focus on your feelings or practice breathing

exercises – take deep breaths in and out slowly. Continue with this and you will fall asleep in no time.

2. **Focus on relaxing rather than sleeping.** If you've found yourself awake again earlier than you intend to, why not focus on relaxing rather than struggling to go back to sleep? Relaxation techniques to try are meditation, visualization, or progressive muscle relaxation all of which can be done without moving from your position on the bed. Although not the same as sleep, relaxation is also energizing and can rejuvenate the body. By relaxing you are likely to fall back to sleep without realising it.
3. **Do not do stimulating activities.** If you have been awake for more than twenty minutes with no hope of going back to bed anytime soon, you should get out of bed and do a non-stimulating activity such as reading. Keep the lights dimmed and don't use screens so as not to send the wrong signal to your body like, 'I think it's time to wake up.'

The effect of RLS is more than the disturbing sensations in the limbs we experience. When dealing with never-ending attacks, we are usually deprived of a whole night's sleep sometimes on a regular basis. Although this lack of sleep can be associated to insomnia, there is a slight difference between insomnia and RLS because what works for insomnia may likely not work RLS.

The following are some tips of what you can do which may improve your chances of getting the natural sleep you deserve. Some are from patients and doctors alike who have a vast combined knowledge and experience in the subject of RLS.

1. Take a hot bath with two cups of Epsom salts containing magnesium. This helps because soaking magnesium into your muscles before going to bed will help loosen the knots and relax them.
2. According to research, taking the amino acid L-tryptophan helps persons with RLS sleep. Food high in tryptophan are chicken, eggs, cheese, turkey, milk, yogurt and pumpkin seeds, to mention but a few.
3. Be careful of the over-the-counter drugs you buy and use because some of these can make RLS worsen. Drugs that are used to treat cold, and allergies, are not very good combination to persons suffering from RLS.
4. Drinking lots of water and eating bananas. In some people, dehydration and low potassium may be a trigger for RLS.
5. Maintain a cool temperature in the room during sleep and be sure to elevate your legs while doing deep-breathing exercises. These strategies may work instead of medications, so why not give it a try?
6. When your legs feel restless and numb, it is best to get out of bed and try to do a calf stretch. Stretch your calves and

the bottom of your feet by kneeling with your hands faced front and toes turned under. Then, you can gradually raise your hands to your thigh and straighten your spine over your sit bones (the lower part of your pelvis that helps you absorb weight when you sit). This exercise will most likely relieve your calves and help you sleep.

7. Put your mind on something creative. Doing an activity which diverts your attention away from the discomfort of RLS, can often do it so well that it becomes easier to ignore the pains. Although it may not be permanent, this method helps to temporarily alleviate the symptoms.
8. Know the ambient temperature which suits you the best whilst sleeping. Do you prefer the room to be cooler or warmer? Try both to see which works best for you.
9. It is good to exercise but you just make sure it's not too much. Exercising to tire your muscles can be helpful and can aid sleep, but too much can also trigger your RLS.
10. In case of the appearance of mild symptoms, you can take pain relief. Ones like Tylenol (Paracetamol) or even Motrin (Ibuprofen) will help you reduce these symptoms.
11. It may be an 'old wives' tale', but it has been reported to work well for some with RLS. Underneath your

bedsheet place an ordinary bar of soap and don't be surprised if you sleep like a baby all night long!

The emphasis of this chapter is that even though you have RLS, it is still possible to sleep well. You lose nothing by trying some or all the tips described above. It is important not to stress or waste too much energy worrying about things out of your control. Focus on what you can do to make things much better for you. At all times, although it is easier said than done, try to stay relaxed.

No-one is asking you to perfect things in a day, it all takes time to find what works for you. The restlessness and sensations in your limbs may prevent you from sleeping and may draw you closer to insomnia, so it is left to you to decide whether to succumb or not. With all the tips above, in addition to time, you should be able to get some sleep and form a good sleep-wake cycle for yourself.

If you feel the information is not enough for you to understand your sleep needs, there are a couple of places where you can download sleep charts and RLS symptom diaries. These may be helpful for you to understand your particular sleep issues due to pain and will provide you with the evidence you may require to show your health professional.

The Restless Legs Syndrome Foundation – RLS Symptom Diary

RLS-UK – My RLS Monitor ™

6

AROMATHERAPY AND ESSENTIAL OILS

Medications are known to help to mitigate the symptoms of RLS whilst not curing it. However, there are some of the millions of sufferers for whom medications alone are not enough to keep it under control. It can be difficult to know what can be used alongside conventional medications to complement their affects and possibly enhance them.

One such complimentary therapy which is natural and has been around for millennia is aromatherapy and the use of essential oils. It was widely used by the Egyptians, Romans, Greeks, other ancient civilisations and during the Elizabethan era. Sadly, the use dropped out until last century when it appeared to rise again and began to be widely used once again.

If you suffer from RLS as I do, you would have probably tried out most of the remedies that are on offer, from over-the-counter patches and heating pads to compresses and hot showers. However, these treatments only bring about temporary relief and as soon as you try and get back to sleep, the urge to move your legs can slowly creep back and you are once again tossing and turning to stop the miserable pulling, twitching, and tugging feelings in your legs. I know your question would be, 'How do or how can essential oils help relieve the symptoms of RLS?'

First, it is important to note that essential oils have several health properties such as anti-neuralgic, analgesic, antispasmodic, calming and sedative effects. Each of these health properties are useful for symptom relief.

Essential oils are natural muscle relaxants and are warming which helps them to perform their roles well and efficiently when treating muscular spasms or aches and pains.

Can aromatherapy and essential oils help cure these uncomfortable sensations? Well, the answer is no. This is because aromatherapy and essential oils are not a cure to RLS. Can essential oils help with RLS? Yes, they can! This is because essential oils are extracted liquids from plants that contain only the essential health qualities or properties of the plant.

Using Carrier oils

There are several health benefits from each of the essential oils and they are each unique and used for different conditions. Essential oils have reported benefits of improving one's mood, promoting relaxation, and relieving pain. However, each of them must be diluted with another oil to prevent allergic reaction or adverse reactions to the specific oil. Some essential oils have very high potency and strength and therefore should be diluted to prevent such skin conditions as contact dermatitis.

These oils are known as carrier oils or bases and include the following:

- Sweet Almond oil
- Fractionated Coconut oil
- Olive oil
- Avocado oil.
- Vitamin E oil
- Castor oil
- Jojoba oil
- Argan oil
- Rosehip oil
- Hemp seed oil
- Apricot Kernel oil
- Calendula oil
- Grapeseed oil
- Pomegranate seed oil

- Neem oil
- Raspberry seed oil
- Wheatgerm virgin oil
- Flax seed virgin oil
- Sesame oil
- Black seed oil
- Moringa oil
- Prickly pear oil
- Cacay oil

These are only some of the available oils used in Aromatherapy. Most vegetable-based oils should be alright to use as a carrier for massage, some oils have a higher viscosity than others. A lighter oil such as sweet almond will be absorbed quite quickly into the skin and is a good starter oil due to its ease of use and reasonable price. Another oil, which may be slightly thicker, will stay for longer on the skin before becoming absorbed, this being ideal for drier skin. If you blend an essential oil with it, start with a weaker solution and make it to the aroma you want by adding more of the essential oil.

The dilution of oils to essential oils for massage are as follows:

To 6 teaspoons of carrier oil add

- 2.5% dilution = 15 drops essential oil (EO)
- 3% dilution = 20 drops EO
- 5% dilution = 30 drops EO

- 10% dilution = 60 drops EO

It is also advised to try a small patch test with the oil before you use it in case you have a reaction to either of the oils.

The Tisserand Institute has made recommendations for the strength of dilution you should put into your bath. They say a rate of 1 – 4% is sufficient and may be made up in the following way. To 10mls (2 tsp) vegetable carrier oil:

- 0.5 % = 1 drop of essential oil (EO)
- 1% = 3 drops EO
- 2% = 6 drops EO
- 3% = 9 drops EO
- 4% = 12 drops EO

However, there are some recipes which specifically use certain other oils and unless you have any allergy to them, they should be used if directed to get the best from the recipe you are trying to emulate.

The Delivery of Aromatherapy.

The really lovely thing about essential oils is the myriad of ways they can be used and delivered.

- **Topically** – use a base oil with your favourite essential oil for massage into the skin or mix with a medium such as an unscented moisture cream.

- **As an inhalation** – add to a diffuser, drop directly on to a cotton wool ball to sniff, add to water as a steam inhalation or add to water in a spray bottle and use as a spray.
- **In bath water** – add a small amount of your oil of choice to a carrier oil and add to the bath. The oils can also be used in making bath bombs and shower melts.
- In a candle to scent your room.

The Oils

As with all the potential reported benefits of the use of essential oils, there are potential side effects. As essential oils differ and vary, so also do the side effects. Here are some of those which are more common for essential oils and aromatherapy:

- When and if applied to the skin without a carrier oil, allergic reactions or contact dermatitis reactions may occur.
- Most should not be taken orally as most essential oils have high active compound concentrations and can cause gastrointestinal disturbance and an allergic reaction may occur.

As a reminder, it is important that before you use any of the essential oils in a topical way, ensure that you dilute it with carrier oil. There are several precautionary steps that you need to take note of when you use essential oils for relieving the symptoms of RLS. They include the following:

- If you suffer from hypertension, are pregnant, or you have epilepsy, you need to avoid Clove and Rosemary oils. Also, ensure that you see a practicing aromatherapist for advice and for questions. This is similar if you are not sure of the essential oils to use and how to use them properly.
- If you are using any essential oils that have citrus in them, ensure that you use them sparingly as they are highly sensitizing to the skin.
- Always ensure that you perform a patch test before you use a new essential oil, so that you can be sure there are no allergic reactions.
- Overuse can cause headaches and dizziness.

Now that we have established what aromatherapy is and how essential oils are vital in relieving RLS, here are some common essential oils that can help relieve you of the symptoms.

The most common essential oils to help reduce muscle spasms and pains are:

- Jasmine
- Rosemary
- Chamomile
- Peppermint.

These are also said to have calming, psychological effects on whoever uses them. For the promotion of sleep and relaxation, the following essential oils are used:

- Cedarwood
- Ylang Ylang
- Marjoram
- Roman Chamomile
- Sandalwood
- Vetiver
- Bergamot
- Lavender

Roman Chamomile Essential Oil

The Roman Chamomile essential oil has anti-neuralgic, analgesic, and antispasmodic properties. This makes it an excellent choice when you need to treat muscle aches and pains. Its naturally calming nature makes it one of the best oils to have to get relief from muscular symptoms. It can be used as a remedy in three ways: as a compress, a massage blend and a hot bath blend.

As a compress:

- Pour four drops of Roman Chamomile into two cups of either hot or cold water.
- Stir the oil through the water and ensure that it mixes.
- Dip a cotton towel into the mix. Wrap the towel

around the parts where you feel the severity of the symptoms.

- Ensure to double the drops of Chamomile when using two cotton towels.

As a massage blend:

- Four drops of Roman Chamomile
- Four drops of Lavender
- Six teaspoons of carrier oil

As a hot bath blend:

- Four drops of Roman Chamomile
- Two drops of Sandalwood
- Two teaspoons of carrier oil

Peppermint Essential Oil

This essential oil has several attributes such as cooling, antispasmodic, and analgesic properties. It offers excellent relief of muscle aches and pains and is an ideal essential oil for relieving RLS. It can be used as a remedy in two ways: as a cold compress and as a massage rub.

As a cold compress:

- Pour four drops of peppermint into two cups of cold

water.

- Add four drops of Yarrow.
- Stir to blend the essential oils smoothly through the water.
- Dip your cotton towel into the water to help absorb the blended mix.
- Wrap your towel around your legs where you feel the symptoms are at its worst.
- If you need to make use of two towels, ensure that you double the recipe.

As a massage rub:

- Two drops of Peppermint
- Four drops of Rosemary
- Four drops of Black Spruce
- Six teaspoons of carrier oil

Marjoram Essential Oil

Marjoram essential oil has sedative, antispasmodic, and analgesic properties. Marjoram is quite useful in relieving muscle spasms and aches and pains. It is also soothing and comforting which makes it an ideal oil for relief. It can be used as a remedy in two ways: as a massage blend and a hot bath blend.

As a massage blend:

- Four drops Marjoram
- Six teaspoons of carrier oil

As a hot bath blend:

- Four drops of Marjoram
- Two drops of Vetiver.
- Two teaspoons of carrier oil.

Lavender Essential Oil

Lavender essential oil is an antispasmodic and analgesic oil essential for relieving muscle spasms, aches, and pains. It also acts as a calming oil to bring deep relaxation, but it can also be uplifting. So, it is a perfect essential oil for relieving both RLS and insomnia. It can be used as a remedy in two ways: as a pain-relieving bath blend or to help relieve insomnia.

As a pain-relieving bath blend:

- Four drops of Lavender
- Two drops of Vetiver
- Two teaspoons of carrier oil

Add to your bath and relax!

To help relieve insomnia:

- Four drops of Lavender
- Two drops of Sweet Orange
- Two teaspoons of carrier oil

Add to your bath and relax!

Vetiver Essential Oil

Vetiver essential oil has calming, sedative and antispasmodic properties. It is an excellent choice when you need to relieve your muscles from strains. It also stimulates the blood circulation giving relief of RLS. Due to its highly calming nature, it is one of the best oils to use for this. It can be used as a remedy in two ways: as a massage blend and a hot bath blend.

As a massage blend:

- Two drops of Vetiver
- Four drops of Linaloe Wood
- Four drops of Neroli
- Six teaspoons of carrier oil

As a hot bath blend:

- Four drops of Sandalwood
- Two drops of Vetiver
- Two teaspoons of carrier oil

Lemongrass Essential Oil

Lemongrass essential oil is a natural sedative with analgesic properties. It can be used as a remedy in two ways: as a massage blend and a diffuser blend.

As a massage blend:

- Two drops of Lemongrass
- Four drops of Ginger
- Four drops of Lavender
- Six teaspoons of carrier oil

As a diffuser blend:

- Four drops of Lavender
- Two drops of Lemongrass

Add to the water in your diffuser, switch on and enjoy!

Frankincense Essential Oil

Frankincense essential oil is a natural sedative and antiseptic. It also promotes balance and deep healing. This makes it a perfect for relieving RLS and for treating insomnia. It can be used as a remedy in two ways: as a pain-relieving bath blend or as a massage blend.

As a pain-relieving bath blend:

- Four drops of Rose Geranium
- Two drops of Frankincense
- Two teaspoons of carrier oil

Add to your bath and enjoy!

As a massage blend:

- Eight drops of Frankincense
- Six teaspoons of carrier oil

Ginger Essential Oil

Ginger essential oil has anti-neuralgic, antispasmodic, and analgesic properties. It is also an essential oil that is useful in the relief of muscle aches and pains with its natural warming property which makes it a great choice as an essential oil to relieve RLS. It can be used as a remedy in two ways: as a hot bath blend or as a massage blend.

As a hot bath blend:

- Two drops of Lavender
- Two drops of Ginger
- Two teaspoons of carrier oil

Add to your bath and enjoy!

As a massage blend:

- Two drops of Ginger
- Four drops of Cardamom
- Four drops of Black Pepper
- Six teaspoons of carrier oil

Jasmine Essential Oil

Jasmine essential oil is a natural antispasmodic and analgesic. It has a rich, sweet floral heady fragrance which appeals to everyone and makes it a perfect oil for relieving RLS. It can be used as a remedy in two ways: as a hot bath blend or as a massage blend.

As a hot bath blend:

- Two drops of Sweet Orange
- Two drops of Jasmine
- Two teaspoons of carrier oil

Add to your bath and enjoy!

As a massage blend:

- Six drops of Jasmine
- Six teaspoons of carrier oil

Rosemary Essential Oil

Rosemary essential oil has antispasmodic, analgesic, and warming properties. It is a natural calming oil and doubles as a natural warming agent. This makes it an ideal therapy for RLS. It can be used as a remedy in several ways two of which are: as a hot bath blend or as a massage blend.

As a hot bath blend:

- Three drops of Lavender
- Two drops of Rosemary
- Two teaspoons of carrier oil

Add to your bath and enjoy!

As a massage blend:

- Four drops of Rosemary
- Four drops of Black Pepper
- Two drops of Vetiver
- Six teaspoons of carrier oil

Black Pepper Essential Oil

Black Pepper essential oil is a natural antispasmodic and analgesic oil with warming properties. It can be used as a remedy in three ways: as a hot bath blend, a diffuser blend or as a massage blend.

As a hot bath blend:

- Two drops of Black Pepper
- Two drops of Jasmine
- Two teaspoons of carrier oil

Add to your bath and relax.

As a massage blend:

- Two drops of Black Pepper
- Four drops of Lavender
- Four drops of Rosemary
- Six teaspoons of carrier oil

As a diffuser blend:

- Three drops of Mandarin
- Two drops of Jasmine

Add to the water in the diffuser and switch on.

Clove Essential Oil

Clove essential oil has natural anti-neuralgic, antispasmodic, and analgesic health properties perfect for muscle relaxation. Clove oil also helps to stimulate the flow of blood in the body.

As a massage blend:

- Six drops of Bergamot
- Two drops of Cinnamon Leaf
- Two drops of Clove
- Six teaspoons of carrier oil

Basil Essential Oil

Basil essential oil is a natural antispasmodic ideal for the relief of muscle spasms and pains.

As a massage blend:

- Four drops of Basil
- Four drops of Lavender
- Two drops of Black Pepper
- Six teaspoons of carrier oil

Bergamot Essential Oil

Bergamot essential oil has natural antispasmodic, analgesic and calming health properties and is an excellent muscle relaxant aiding relief for RLS. It can be used as a remedy in two ways: as a hot bath blend and as a massage blend.

As a hot bath blend:

- Two drops of Bergamot

- Two drops of Neroli
- Two teaspoons of carrier oil

Add to your bath, sit back, and relax!

As a massage blend:

- Two drops of Bergamot
- Four drops of Sandalwood
- Four drops of Jasmine
- Six teaspoons of carrier oil

Yarrow Essential Oil

Yarrow essential oil has natural anti-neuralgic, antispasmodic, and analgesic health properties. It also acts as an anti-inflammatory agent and this important quality makes it a powerful oil. It can be used as a remedy in two ways: as a massage oil and as a cold or hot compress.

As a massage oil:

- Six drops of Yarrow
- Four tablespoons of carrier oil
- Six teaspoons of carrier oil

As a hot or cold compress:

- Blend four drops of Yarrow.

- Add two cups of cold or hot water.
- Stir the oil through the water to mix properly.
- Dip in your cotton towel into the water so that it absorbs the liquid.
- Wrap a towel around the leg or parts where you feel the symptoms are the worst.
- Double the recipe if you want to use two towels.

If you want a combination of essential oils for relief, here are three recipes that are effective:

Night-Time Cream - This recipe has four ingredients:

- Two ounces of plain lotion or cream.
- Five drops of Roman Chamomile oil
- Ten drops of Marjoram oil
- Twelve drops of Lavender oil.

To use: completely blend all the ingredients into a jar measuring two ounces and apply it right before going to sleep or to bed. This helps you gain some much-needed relief before settling.

Travel Spray - This is also four ingredients:

- Lavender hydrosol (gelatinous liquid form)
- Eight drops of Siberian Fir oil
- Eight drops of Sweet Orange
- Nine drops of Petitgrain oil.

To use: thoroughly mix all the ingredients into a spray bottle measuring two ounces and spray it on the areas that you have or feel discomfort, at any part of the day.

Bath Salts - This is of five ingredients:

- Himalayan pink salt
- Three drops of Ylang Ylang oil
- Five drops of Clary Sage oil
- Five drops of Marjoram oil
- Ten drops of Frankincense oil.

To use: mix these ingredients in a jar measuring two ounces and use it as a bath salt. When next you take your bath before going to bed, use the oil blend for some relief.

You can mix your own blends of essential oils. One of the blends you can easily make or mix on your own is the topical or transdermal magnesium oil for RLS.

Making your own Magnesium sprays.

Pinterest gives some helpful advice as to their use and some excellent recipes. The recipe below is from Omnomally.com: Ingredients/supplies.

1. 250ml water
2. 1 cup Magnesium Chloride flakes.
3. 10 drops lavender EO.

4. 5 drops marjoram EO.
5. 5 drops ylang ylang EO.

Preparation

1. Pour water into a small saucepan and bring to the boil, then removing from the heat.
2. Stir in the Magnesium flakes continuously until they dissolve completely.
3. Cool to room temperature.
4. When cool enough, add the essential oils and mix to combine everything.
5. Use a funnel to pour the mixture into one or more spray bottles.
6. Use as required and massage into affected areas.
7. Store in a cool and dark place.

Making an Epsom bath foot soak.

This is one of the easiest methods of relieving stress in one's muscles. You only need the most basic of ingredients to begin with

- One cup Epsom salt (magnesium sulphate)
- Basin of warm water.

Add the Epsom salts and stir until dissolved. Soak your feet for at least fifteen minutes in the evening, preferably before bed.

This should help to remove toxins, and help you sleep better. Pinterest has many recipes and variations of this to help from sleeplessness to cracked heels and is worth visiting for ideas.

Further recipes you may find useful

Sometimes you will see recipes which involve roller ball bottles. These usually come in 10ml, but size and colour of the bottles can vary depending on their use and can be as large as 50mls. These are particularly useful if you make an oil blend to dab on sore or painful points and want to carry it around for ease of use. Below are some further recipes which may be helpful to you in trying to control symptoms.

Deep Sleep
10 drops Lavender
5 drops Vetiver
6 drops Frankincense
Place in a 10ml roller bottle
And fill the rest with carrier oil.

From www.coloryourhealth.com

Sleep Tight
2 drops Bergamot
2 drops lavender
2 drops vetiver
2 drops Cedarwood
Place in a 10ml roller bottle
And fill the rest with carrier oil.
from www.paintedteacup.com

Roller recipes for pain relief.

'Morphine' Bomb (No actual morphine included!)

Into a 10ml roller ball bottle put:

15 drops lavender
15 drops peppermint
10 drops chamomile
10 drops marjoram
10 drops lemongrass.

Fill the rest of the bottle with your chosen carrier oil and shake well. Roll on to the affected area as required from Essential oils US. I have to say, this is one of my favourites and seems to work for me.

'Muscle Soreness Relief'

10 drops Lemongrass EO
5 drops Peppermint EO
10 drops Copaiba EO
5 drops Wintergreen.

Add to a 10ml rollerball bottle and top up with a carrier oil of your choice.

'Pain-Away Roll-on blend'

5 drops copaiba
3 drops Marjoram
3 drops Basil
3 drops Frankincense

Add to a 10ml rollerball bottle and top up with carrier oil of your choice.

(A Less toxic life)

Energy and Mood Boosting Essential Oil Blends for a Diffuser.

Below are some of the best blends for your home diffuser which will help you to gain more energy and lift your mood. No need to add a carrier oil here, the amount of water in the diffuser acts as this. Just add the drops and switch on. Give them a try.

1. Thyme 1 drop, Tangerine 3 drops.
2. Grapefruit 3 drops, Orange 2 drops, Lime 1 drop.
3. Lemon 3 drops, Basil 3 drops, Peppermint 2 drops, Lime 2 drops.
4. Orange 2 drops, Lemongrass 2 drops, Wintergreen 2 drops.
5. Lavender 2 drops, Lemon 2 drops, Rosemary 2 drops.
6. Bergamot 3 drops, Cypress 1 drop.

7. Ylang Ylang 2 drops, Orange 2 drops, Lavender 2 drops.
8. Patchouli 2 drops, Orange 3 drops, Ylang 2 drops.
9. Tangerine 3 drops, Dill 1 drop, Lime 1 drop.
10. Grapefruit 4 drops, Rosemary 3 drops, Peppermint 3 drops.
11. Orange 4 drops, Ylang Ylang 2 drops, Bergamot 2 drops.
12. Grapefruit 2 drops, Lemon 2 drops, Peppermint 1 drop.
13. Lavender 3 drops, Rosemary 1 drop.
14. Lemon 3 drops, Basil 3 drops, Lime 2 drops.
15. Geranium 1 drop, Grapefruit 1 drop, Lemon 2 drops.
16. Rosemary 2 drops, Cypress 2 drops, Juniper 2 drops.
17. Lavender 1 drop, Frankincense 2 drops, Bergamot 3 drops.
18. Rosemary 2 drops, Peppermint 2 drops, Lemon 2 drops.
19. Tangerine 4 drops, Lavender 2 drops, Lime 1 drop, Spearmint 1 drop.
20. Lavender 1 drop, Clary Sage 2 drops, Bergamot 3 drops.
21. Orange 3 drops, Ginger 1 drop, Frankincense 2 drops.
22. Orange 3 drops, Grapefruit 1 drop, Lemon 2 drops, Bergamot 1 drop.
23. Orange 3 drops, Peppermint 3 drops.

24. Cedarwood 2 drops, Lavender 2 drops, Vetiver 2 drops.
25. Geranium 1 drop, Tangerine 2 drops.
26. Vetiver 2 drops, Peppermint 2 drops, Lemon 2 drops.

The following oils should be used with caution if you are pregnant, nursing or have children under 10.

> Sage, Peppermint, Spearmint, Rosemary, Dill, Lemongrass, Wintergreen.

In this chapter, I have discussed the use of Aromatherapy and essential oils in the homeopathic treatment of RLS. I must admit, this is an area I enjoy very much, and I have tinkered quite a lot to find some recipes of roll-ons and topical oils to help with pain and discomfort. Therefore, I have a lot of them! I like to put them into the atomiser to fragrance a room and use an uplifting oil such as grapefruit, orange and lime or vetiver or lemon and peppermint which lifts one's mood and can give you a little more energy. I also have put them into bath bombs, shower melts, and loo cleaning blocks! Their versatility is amazing.

It is important to know that these little bottles of aroma are potent, and have the ability of lifting your mood, soothing pain, helping you sleep, giving you energy and calming you. The benefits are endless. I have found them particularly useful to abate the side effects of my RLS, and my Fibromyalgia.

However, it is important to know the safety side of the oils. Some such as Basil, Camphor, Cedarwood, Cinnamon, Clove, Fennel, Juniper berry, horseradish, mustard, nutmeg, Rosemary and Wintergreen are not to be used whilst pregnant. There are also certain oils which can affect your pets if they are used in atomisers in the home. There are many oils toxic to dogs, too many to mention here, but very easily found by doing a Google search, and this also goes for cats and children (should I have put the children first?) I have only given you an overview of using essential oils, you will still need to do some homework. If you do, I hope you enjoy researching and using them as much as I have done, and still do.

For further information, The National Center for Complementary and Integrative Health in the USA has considered aromatherapy a vital intervention and over the years, aromatherapy has increased in popularity once more. While there are not federally approved uses of these interventions for a specific illness, aromatherapy has been used to treat health disorders and conditions for centuries. In the UK and worldwide the International Federation of Aromatherapists (IFA) holds a register of all registered aromatherapists.

7

ALTERNATIVE THERAPIES AND DEVICES

Some RLS sufferers cannot take drugs to alleviate their symptoms, pregnant ladies being one which comes to mind. Unfortunately, their conditions do not stop them from feeling the intense pain and discomfort caused by RLS. In some cases, medications require a helping hand for significant effectiveness. For these reasons, alternative and complementary treatments for RLS are useful, especially for those with severe symptoms.

Drug free alternative treatments have proven to be of great help. Although some of them are not medically proven, users have testified to their effectiveness. It is these therapies, devices and topical products which will be discussed in this chapter. Some have proven to help a great deal in the symptoms and others have not. This is not to say one of the below will be of help to you, sometimes, you just must give it a go.

Acupuncture

Although controversial for many years among Western medical specialists and doctors, acupuncture remains one of the most commonly used therapies for RLS. In recent years, an increasing number of studies have been published in favour of the effectiveness of acupuncture for RLS. A study conducted in 2015 by Weidong *et al* on thirty-one people with RLS who were treated with acupuncture for six weeks, showed a reduction in their abnormal leg activities

Acupuncture is an inherent part of Traditional Chinese Medicine (TCM) which has been in existence for over 2000 years. It is an age-long form of treatment which involves inserting very tiny needles through a person's skin at distinct and specific points. Acupuncture is primarily used to relieve pain but has also been used in the treatment of other conditions. However, the National Center for Complementary and Integrated Health (NCCHI) argue there is a lack of sufficient evidence for its effectiveness in treating conditions other than pain. This form of treatment is popular in countries like France, UK, and America. According to the British Acupuncture Council, about 2.3 million acupuncture treatments are given each year.

It is well known that traditional Chinese medicine advocates acupuncture as a method used for balancing the flow of energy (chi) believed to flow to the meridians of the body. Western practitioners, however, believe that acupuncture helps to stimulate muscles, nerves, and connective tissues. According to

NCCHI, acupuncture has proven effective in the treatment of headache and migraine, knee pain, neck pain, low back pain and osteoarthritis. Acupuncture is a potential alternative for pain medication and can be used as a complementary treatment in severe cases. To determine the type of acupuncture that will help you, your acupuncturist will ask you about your symptoms, carry out an examination and assess your condition. Acupuncture appointments take between about 30 minutes to an hour in most cases. For RLS, manual acupuncture, electroacupuncture or warm needle acupuncture is often the mode of treatment.

I have used this treatment for some time and have found that when my legs are severe a few sessions with my acupuncturist helps a great deal. I highly recommend this form of treatment. For me it is effective and does give me some relief between treatments for my legs. This may be an issue for those who have a phobia against needles, but the treatment is mostly painless (you don't usually feel anything unless the needle is placed in an area of particular soreness) and strangely relaxing. Sessions near me in Hampshire are around £42 but some practitioners may offer a bundle deal of six sessions for the price of 5 which is much more economical if you intend to carry the treatment forward. Initially, if you are uncertain about the treatment, pay for a one-off session.

Massage

Many people have found relief from their symptoms with consistent leg massage before bed. Health organizations such as the National Institute of Health, recommends it as an at-home treatment. Habitual leg massage in addition to other RLS treatments have proven to be effective and safe. It not only improves circulation of blood, but also promotes relaxation which could help improve sleep.

Ideally, one should massage one's legs for thirty to sixty minutes at least twice a week. The National Institute of Neurological Disorders and Stroke (USA) claims that RLS may be related to poor circulation. Therefore, seeing a licensed massage therapist for a massage to put enough pressure on the affected areas to aid the easy movement of blood through the veins is a profitable idea for those with RLS.

In 2007 a case study of a 35-year-old woman with RLS had 45-minute leg massages twice a week for three weeks. During this time she kept diaries of her sleeping habits and pain from her RLS which illustrated the benefits of massaging the leg muscles. Her massages included several techniques, including Swedish massage and direct pressure to leg muscles. Her RLS symptoms were said to have improved after two treatments until weeks after the massage treatment ended.

Leg massage is beneficial to both mild and severe RLS patients, however, it may be advisable to speak to your doctor for his approval.

Exercise

Any movement that makes one's muscles work and burn calories is an exercise. The National Institute of Health has confirmed that moderate exercise may help relieve mild RLS symptoms. The reason for this is not far-fetched as exercises helps blood circulation, relaxation and improvement of sleep and brain function.

A starting point of thirty-sixty minutes of mild exercise is beneficial because experts agree that intense exercise, especially before bedtime may have an adverse impact. The Restless Legs Foundation also recommends moderation in exercise. Walking, jogging, swimming, cycling, dancing, stair climbing and so on are types of exercise.

As mentioned previously any kind of movement is good, but you do need to actively carry out these movements. Plan to do them, create a routine for yourself and stick to it. It does not matter if you are only walking around the block once a day, it is a start. You can build from there.

Many of us during the lockdowns of 2020/21 have gained a few extra pounds which we need to shift now we are allowed to carry on our daily living to almost normal standards. It is OK to go to the park and walk, meet friends and family. Why not make it a group activity?

Yoga

Yoga is an ancient philosophy from India. It has been used for thousands of years but is a practice which still has relevance today. The word 'Yoga' is a Sanskrit word meaning 'union'. Many of us seek a higher state of awareness and undertaking the practice of yoga meditation can bring a tangible understanding of the meaning of our lives and a way of guiding our development. So, this is not a practice of just sitting in various poses, there is much more to it than that.

Yoga masters were known in the past to impose a rigid discipline over their students to aid their overcoming of vices such as ego and 'conditionings'. When free from these burdens, seekers were able to receive self-realisation which was a state of inner stillness, heightened awareness and joy – this was known as Yoga.

Yoga has a side effect of improving our lives, reducing stress and worries, health and relationships and heightening joy and satisfaction in our lives.

Yoga and stretching exercises (calf, front thigh, and hip) have also proven to be beneficial in improving symptoms. It has also been shown to be another activity which reduces the symptoms and improves sleep. It does this by using deep breathing, stretching and relaxation to increase blood flow. In 2013 Kim

Innes *et al* carried out an eight-week pilot study of 10 women who suffered from RLS. The women ranged in age from 32-66 and were asked to attend classes and do some yoga at home, increasing the time they practiced gradually over the sessions. The findings were only preliminary; however, they did suggest as well as relieving symptoms, it aided sleep and help to reduce stress and mood issues.

There are also known to be other benefits of yoga:

1. Improvement in posture
2. Increase in flexibility
3. Builds muscle strength
4. Boosts metabolism
5. Helps to lower blood sugar
6. Increases blood flow
7. Increases self-esteem
8. May boost immunity

Compression

Compression increases the flow of blood which consequently increases oxygen levels in the tissue reducing muscle contraction and nerve sensation as in RLS. Compression therapy is an easy way to alleviate RLS symptoms.

In the case of a compression socks, one between the range of 15-20mmHg range can relieve the restless sensation in RLS patients. These elastic socks are worn to apply pressure to the legs and ankles increasing circulation. If you want to try this type of treatment, it is preferable to speak to your doctor or GP practice nurse specialising in this area. It may not be possible to get some of the types of stockings /socks on the NHS, but they will be available to you online.

Graduated compression knee high socks provide the right amount of pressure in the correct places and helps to reduce the swelling in legs and improve circulation. They do not need to be worn all the time, they can be used just in the evening when resting as an alternative to all day, although this is fine too.

They come in different colours and so long as you check the product sizing chart for the correct fit, there is something to suit all occasions.

Foot wraps, just like compression socks, apply pressure to the muscles around the legs. The revolutionary foot wrap that applies gentle, relieving pressure to certain muscles in the foot, thereby reducing irritating impulses in the legs is known as Restiffic. It is a drug-free device which includes two-foot wraps that go around the centre of each foot. Restiffic is a therapy that helps by relaxing the muscles affected by RLS, relieving its symptoms. In 2013, a study of 30 people who used Restiffic foot wrap for eight weeks discovered significant amelioration of RLS and an improvement in sleep quality.

Meditation

Meditation is a practice that allows an individual to focus on a particular object, thought or activity and achieve mental clarity, stability, and emotional calmness. It uses a technique known as mindfulness to achieve this.

Exercises involves deep inhalation and exhalation and is good for tackling stress and symptoms of RLS. One should practice this daily for around 20 – 30 minutes usually in the morning on an empty stomach. It may not be possible to do this for more than 5 -10 minutes initially, however one should be able to carry it out for half an hour a day.

There has been insufficient study carried out on the effect of meditation and mindfulness on RLS, however, there has been plenty on the effectiveness of meditation in brain function and stress levels which are both important in the treatment of RLS.

Drink Chamomile, Green or Parsley Tea

If you have fresh Chamomile, you can boil your water and add a few leaves to the water. Leave for about ten minutes before you strain it and drink. It helps to calm and sooth your senses. A cup of green tea is an affective alternative.

Parsley tea can be an effective reliever of those horrible creepy crawly symptoms one can feel. It is full of the minerals so important for health such as calcium, iron, potassium, magnesium, and manganese. The vitamins in this wonder plant are

B1, B2, B3, B5, B6, A, E, C, K, and antioxidants. It is also known for its antiseptic and anaesthetic properties and helps to absorb all nutrients such as iron and calcium.

To make the tea is very easy:

1. Take a cup of water in a saucepan and put in a teaspoon of parsley.
2. Boil the water for a few minutes.
3. Allow the water to simmer down and then strain the tea. Voila!

The tea can be further enhanced by adding honey or lemon, whichever is preferred. This tea should be taken up to three times a day until the twitching dies down. Eating calcium rich foods may make the twitching return, so try to reduce this intake.

Apple Cider Vinegar

This is a common item found in the home used for killing weeds, pickling and even polishing silver. It's also good over a salad! Did you know it can also be very beneficial to those suffering RLS? It is something else which is packed with calcium, potassium, magnesium, phosphorus, copper, and vitamins. The vitamins included are B1, B2, B6, A, E, C, bioflavonoids, and pectin. The absorption of such vitamins and minerals is further aided by the acetic acid of the vinegar. To help with the symptoms:

1. Take a cup of warm water and a teaspoon of apple cider vinegar and combine.
2. Drink slowly before retiring to bed about half an hour beforehand.
3. Take this daily.

It is also possible to use the vinegar to massage into one's legs before bed. It will aid the twitchiness. Of course, you will smell slightly of fermenting apples, but it will gradually fade.

Coconut Oil

Coconut oil is well known for its health benefits. I am not sure that there has been much research into the use of it for restless legs, however there is nothing to lose by trying it, especially if you were going to massage your legs anyway.

1. Warm a teaspoon of oil very slightly.
2. Massage into your limbs applying a gentle pressure.
3. Massage in circles from your ankles to your knees.
4. Do this twice daily to help to mitigate symptoms.

Hot and cold treatments

Hot or cold baths and hot or cold compresses have for so long been home remedies for various conditions including, muscle pull, inflammation, swelling, and arthritis. Whether to use hot or cold treatment depends on how your body reacts. If a warm bath or a hot compress aggravates your symptoms, then you should try the reverse or what seems to work for you.

Reflexology

This is a type of massage in which different amounts of pressure is applied to the hands, feet, and ears. This technique is based on the theory that those three body parts are connected to specific organs and body systems. According to traditional Chinese medicine qi (pronounced 'Chee') is blocked. Qi is the vital energy each of us has flowing through them. The practice of reflexology keeps the qi flowing and therefore, keeps the body in balance. When it is out of balance, this is when one is prone to illness. All the parts of the body have a corresponding point on the feet, hands, and ears. It is at these points pressure should be applied to bring the qi back into balance. The touch of the reflexologist helps to relax, reduce stress and pain, relieving tired feet, and improving overall well-being.

Reflexology may help in easing symptoms; however, it is not a scientifically proven treatment. It is very much subjective, and one would need to try it to see whether it does have any effects on the relief of RLS symptoms.

Reiki

Reiki means universal or spiritual life force energy. It is a Japanese energy healing therapy which appeared around the late 1800s, that hastens the body's healing process by activating its ability to heal itself. It works on the postulation that the human body is an energy vessel, connected to all living things in the universe. This therapy is carried out by a Reiki practitioner.

According to wellness Lab in 2020, Reiki can help RLS in four main ways which includes: regulating dopamine levels, improving sleep, unblocking all energy pathways, and promoting relaxation. Like reflexology, this is not a scientifically proven therapy, but many hospitals have embraced its benefits and will offer treatment to its patients as a complementary therapy.

The practitioner does not touch the patient but rather hovers their hands over the patient and 'transfers' energy to the patient through their hands. This may take between two and five minutes and involves the practitioner making different hand shapes to channel the energy.

Patients have described the treatments as very relaxing, reducing stress and even falling asleep. They state the practitioners' hands became quite hot!

Hypnotherapy

Hypnotherapy is the use of hypnosis as a therapeutic technique to enhance relaxation and treat specific symptoms and conditions. This therapy allows a person to focus on inner experiences rather than outer awareness to aid treatment. Research shows that it helps with dementia, irritable bowel syndrome, childbirth pain and psoriasis, among others.

According to London Hypnotherapy, UK, RLS responds well to hypnotherapy. The deep form of relaxation that comes with the treatment allows the patient to oppose the uncomfortable feelings in their legs. RLS patients are encouraged to learn self-hypnosis and use it daily at home.

Ayurvedic treatment

Ayurvedic medicine or Ayurveda is one of the world's oldest holistic (whole body) medical systems. It is the oldest traditional healing system in India having been developed over 3000 years ago. It is based upon a natural and holistic approach to mental and physical health. The promotion of good health is its main message and rather than fight disease and illness, it targets treatment toward specific health problems and needs. Its treatment is a combination of products (plants, animals, metal and mineral), diet, therapies and lifestyle for the treatment and prevention of illnesses, defence against diseases and cleansing of the mind, body, and spirit.

Practitioners of Ayurveda have a belief that we are all made from the five basic elements of air, fire, earth, water, and space. They also believe we are all connected to the universe and exist in harmony with it. We become ill when the balance shifts and something is 'off'.

The elements come together within the body to form energies called doshas. These influence how your body functions and are:

Vata dosha – space and air
Pitta dosha – fire and water
Kapha dosha – water and earth

We each are made of a mix of the above each controlling a function of the body, Ayurveda believes you will become ill if they become imbalanced.

Ayurvedic practitioners believe RLS occurs due to the imbalance of Vata Dosha, therefore it is this imbalance which must be treated. A neurological disorder called Grindhrasi shows many of the same symptoms of RLS with the characteristic stiffness, pain, and prickling sensations. Therefore, the treatment for both is very similar.

Note that Ayurvedic practice is not regulated in the US and there are few centres for treatment. The treatments are considered forms of complementary and alternative medicine (CAM). The U.S. Food and Drug Administration points out the potential harmfulness of metal, mineral or gem in Ayurvedic preparations. Cases of lead poisoning due to Ayurvedic medication have also been reported in Victoria, Australia. Therefore, contact your doctor for approval of Ayurvedic treatment before commencement. On the other hand, Ayurvedic is a recognized treatment in the UK. There is an Ayurvedic centre in London where holistic treatments are administered.

Cannabis

In recent times, Cannabis, also known as Marijuana, has been recognized by many experts as a potential treatment for various diseases and health conditions including RLS. New evidence suggests that cannabidiol (CBD) may be helpful in relieving RLS symptoms. While inhaling Marijuana may give rapid relief of symptoms, tinctures, and edibles (micro-dosing) are suggested for long lasting relief.

Medical cannabis for RLS acts on the brain's cannabinoid receptors to give psychoactive effect in areas of coordination, motor activity and pain relief.

Although, there is a lack of sufficient medical evidence on the use of cannabis to treat RLS symptoms, anecdotal evidence for the treatment of RLS symptoms with cannabis is on the increase. However, your care provider should be contacted for medical go-ahead and proper dose before commencing the use of cannabis.

In the UK this is tightly regulated and stringently enforced. There are clinics who can offer treatment using Cannabis, but one must be under the care of a doctor and be referred to the clinic. These consultations will be treated as private and will incur a cost. If prescribing through the NHS, the doctor to prescribe must be a specialist on the General Medical Council

Register and then the decision to prescribe is further agreed by a multidisciplinary team. A GP can make a referral to a doctor who is on this list when the patient has tried all else.

In a study on Sleep, Pain and Cannabis published in the 2015 edition of the *Journal of Sleep Disorders and Therapy,* the researchers acknowledged the abilities of cannabis to relieve pain and promote sleep. Another study in 2017 of six RLS patients who used Cannabis to relieve RLS symptoms, five patients reported a near total disappearance of symptoms while one spoke of complete disappearance of symptoms and improved sleep quality.

It is noteworthy that the growing, possession, distribution and sale of cannabis is illegal in UK and USA. It has only been made legal for medical use in the UK and for medical and recreational use in the U.S. Therefore, I don't endorse its use. It is included in the book for information and education purposes, but it is left to the reader to decide whether to take the risk of pursuing its use.

Topical treatments

The topical application of products can also help in relieving RLS symptoms when applied over the skin. They include oils, creams and gels and are explained below:

Oils, Creams and Gels

Essential oils have been discussed at length in Chapter 6.

Arnica Care gel/cream - is a non-greasy gel that is quickly absorbed by the body to give temporary relief to muscle pains caused by overexertion, falls and minor injuries. This gel/cream may help in reducing RLS symptom because it improves blood circulation and relieves leg pains. It is natural and can be purchased from chemists, pharmacies, and health food shops. Manufacturers and proponents of this product also state that it is as affective as ibuprofen gel. I think it works as well too.

CBD oil - is also suggested for alleviating RLS symptoms. This oil is obtained from industrial hemp, which contains a higher amount of cannabidiol, but is free of tetrahydrocannabinol (THC), which is the psychoactive agent that creates the feeling of excitement in the user. Therefore, if it is less than 0.3% THC, it is legal at a federal level in the USA and can be purchased, but it may still be illegal under some state laws. Marijuana- derived CBD products are still illegal at federal level but are still legal under some state laws. The strength of the oil depends on the manufacturer and can be as high as 7,500mg per 30ml. However, the lower strengths are advised as a starting point and one should work up to a strength which gives the benefits one needs. It should also be noted that the lower dosed bottles are less expensive than those of a higher dose, however, it may be that a larger bottle with a greater strength may be more economical. This can be purchased from reputable sellers online, but the FDA has also shown that there are sometimes inaccuracies on the labels of such items which can be misleading.

In the UK CBD oil can be purchased in many different formats. It can come as a capsule, dropper, gummy or spray. The dosage can be very confusing as different manufacturers display different information on their labels and may be as a percentage or as mg. The strengths may be shown as from 5 – 30% or 300mg – 1500mg. The liquid comes in either a 10ml or 30 ml bottle and price vary greatly depending on composition of the oil, its intended use and the quality of the ingredients. Whichever you choose, make sure the manufacturer states it has been 'third party tested'. The Independent on-line carried out a research into which are the best CBD oils.

Hemp pain relief cream - is another a type of CBD cream that helps with a variety of pain sensations including RLS pains. Personally, I have tried it. It is less heating than other topical creams such as 'Deep Heat', and it doesn't smell as strongly. It is warming and soothing and I found it quite beneficial as well as relatively cost effective.

Kratom

Whilst carrying out my research for this book, I came across this substance I had not heard of before. Kratom is derived from the Kratom tree growing in SE Asia. It is not under international control; however, it has been banned in the UK under the Psychoactive Substances Act since 2016.

Kratom is usually in the form of a greenish powder and is named after a colour of the veins in the leaves of the tree or from the region in which it is grown. It is taken orally and produces affects not unlike that of opium. However, considerably large amounts would have to be consumed to reach these effects and anecdotal evidence shows that much lower doses can have a positive effect of lessening pain and fatigue. Whilst it does not appear to cause any respiratory suppression, it has been cited in cases of tachycardia, agitation, constipation, nausea, and vomiting.

In 2016, the Drug Enforcement Administration (DEA) in the US expressed a wish to put this onto a schedule making the possession and use of it illegal. However, there was an overwhelming response to this. Marches and petitions took place including both users and members of the medical profession. As far as I am aware, Kratom is yet to be scheduled.

As previously stated, I don't endorse the use of such drugs, the risk is entirely up to you!

Devices

Most of the treatments we have discussed so far do not involve any equipment as such, but it should be said, there are useful devices on the market nowadays which are extremely useful in helping to calm and relieve RLS symptoms. We shall talk about these in the next section.

Relaxis vibrating pad.

Vibrating pads are basically used for improving blood circulation. In the case of RLS, a vibrating pad called Relaxis, was the first medically approved device by the Food and Drug Administration (FDA) for RLS treatment in the US in June 2014. The theory behind this pad is to provide a 'counter stimulation' through vibration, that interrupts the uncomfortable sensations in your legs, caused by RLS, thereby making you feel the vibrations instead of your symptoms.

In the US, the Relaxis is a prescription device that includes a pillow sized pad that vibrates at different intensities. The pads come in 3 sizes and can be battery-operated or plugged in. The pad is placed under the legs and is activated and controlled through a connected controller with which you adjust the intensity of the vibration and how long you want it to vibrate. It shuts down gradually after 30 minutes without waking the user.

While there is not enough research available on Relaxis pad, two clinical trials have demonstrated that the Relaxis pad provides notable sleep improvement compared to improvement seen in RLS drug trials. A study also found it to be as effective in improving sleep as the four FDA approved drugs were. (See chapter 2)

The Relaxis pad is a good option for those with mild RLS who are unable to take the usual prescribed drugs but is not advisable for people with deep vein thrombosis (DTV). For those with more pronounced symptoms it is used alongside other medications.

As an amendment to this section according to SleepReview-mag.com prescriptions for the device are no longer being filled. This is because the Centers for Medicare and Medicaid Services (CMS), have categorised the device as a 'pleasure device' and so is not eligible for coverage by prescription. It may be possible to find something similar on Amazon or via another manufacturer.

Revitive

Revitive is a drug-free clinically proven circulation booster that uses patented Electrical Muscle Stimulation (EMS) to boost circulation in legs and feet to relieve pain. The EMS gets the muscle in the feet and calf pumping, thereby drawing fresh and rich oxygenated blood into your feet while returning waste carbon-dioxide back to the heart through the veins. Revitive helps in improving circulation, reducing pains and cramp, and reducing swollen feet and ankles. It may help in reducing the symptoms of RLS. This is readily available from online stores, and high street stores and is an alternative to the Relaxis because it doesn't need a prescription.

Electroacupuncture (EA)

This is a modified form of acupuncture that requires two needles, an electropuncture machine and electrodes instead of one needle used in the former. In the case of electroacupuncture, a mild electric current pass between these needles during treatment, applying more stimulation to acupoints. It is intended to improve the healing effects of standard acupuncture as they are used to treat similar conditions. It takes about 10-20 minutes which is less than the time taken for standard acupuncture.

Electroacupuncture is a comparatively recent therapy, which is why there isn't much evidence to support its effectiveness. However, a study in 2020 on the effect of electroacupuncture on RLS in haemodialysis patients hypothesize that EA can help patients improve the abnormal leg activity in haemodialysis patients with RLS. They suggest it is an effective alternative in terms of cost and safety.

Like acupuncture, electroacupuncture is safe when performed by a skilled acupuncturist. Those who have a bleeding disorder, pregnant women and people with pacemakers should contact their healthcare provider before have electroacupuncture.

As a side note, I have used this along with acupuncture and it is a slightly weird feeling with the needles pulsating very slightly. It doesn't hurt, but neither does acupuncture and if it is offered to you as part of the main appointment, go with it. I found that it really does enhance the success of the treatment.

Near-Infrared Spectroscopy (NIRS)

NIRS is a painless, non-invasive treatment that uses light beams. The idea behind this treatment is to stimulate blood flow in the muscles and increase circulation by emitting light beams for the near-infrared light device. It is though that NIRS increases oxygen levels, thereby relieving RLS symptoms.

Treatment is undertaken by sticky pads being applied to one's legs, or this may be a small light-emitting device. A light of a particular wavelength then passes through one's skin thereby increasing oxygen flow. It is not harmful, but it may warm the surface of the skin slightly. It is not known whether this treatment works better on male or female subjects, or even primary or secondary RLS, therefore more studies need to be carried out to establish this.

As this treatment is a form of phototherapy, it also increases the endorphins in the brain which are natural chemicals which relieve pain. There are no drugs involved and this is classed as a complementary therapy,

Transcutaneous Electrical Nerve Stimulation (TENS)

TENS involves applying electric current on the skin through electrodes to control pain. This current is produced by a battery-operated device that is usually connected to the skin through two or more sticky pads - electrodes. The idea behind this device is of 'counter stimulation' like the Relaxis pad.

Using the TENS device for 15-30 minutes daily using low voltage electrical current may help reduce RLS symptoms. A study showed that a patient with RLS-like symptoms experienced complete symptoms relief with regular use of TENS combined with vibration.

These devices are readily available from internet stores and can be purchased for a few pounds/dollars. It is important to purchase a TENS machine which is NOT for labour. Neither should the type used for during labour be used for general pain. These are two different devices.

Weighted blanket

This is a blanket that contains weighted balls or pellets and works similarly to the Deep Pressure Stimulation (DPS) Technique. It provides a firm and gentle pressure to the muscles of the body, relaxing them and increasing circulation. Weighted blanket claims to work for anxiety, depression, ADHD, insomnia and even RLS.

Some cannot tolerate the weight of such a blanket which ranges from two to thirty-six pounds. Others claim the weight and the pressure from the blanket could provide some stimulation to the legs that might replace the need to move the leg to relieve that restless sensation, leaving a therapeutic calming effect.

There is no scientific evidence to support the claims of a weighted blanket as a home remedy for relieving RLS symptom, however, this blanket helps in improving sleep patterns.

I am a member of many Facebook groups which have a link to RLS. Many of the members support the use of these blankets, however, buyer beware! Manufacturers state that the weight of your blanket should amount to around ten percent of your own weight. Now, I am not the smallest of ladies, I never have been, so ten percent of my weight is a sizeable amount! I followed this advice and purchased a double blanket which weighs as much as a body – literally, a body! Trying to drag that around the house is exhausting and I have to ask my husband to help. He is currently fighting cancer and so exhausts as easily as I do. We are totally f******d by the time I get it to where I want it. We have agreed it stays upstairs on the day bed. If I need it, I use it there. Heaven only knows how the courier managed to lug it to my door!

In this chapter, we reviewed various therapies, devices and topical products which have helped in alleviating or treating RLS. Some of these treatments have medical or scientific backings while other have just anecdotal evidence of their effectiveness in treatment. While some of these treatments require spending some money, others are completely free.

I am unable to say which of them, if any, will successfully work for you. However, I have made it my mission to try as many complimentary therapies as I can to try to alleviate this horrible syndrome for myself. I admit, not all of them have worked for me, but some have been relatively successful, and others work very well. I will have to leave it to you to try any of the above and see whether they work for your symptoms. You may wish to consult with your physician or GP if you are not sure about their use.

As a further note, RLS-UK has developed a means of tracking your RLS symptoms and spots patterns in attacks. It is called My RLS Monitor ™ It can be downloaded here or see below.

8

I CAN'T COPE, I WANT TO END IT!

For some of us, the RLS symptoms we experience are horrendous, destroy our quality of life, and bring us so low it would seem that to end one's life is the only alternative. Sleep deprivation and depression are something we are constantly at odds with. Individuals with RLS have nearly three times the tendency to commit suicide and self-harm which is strongly associated with depression, sleep disorders, chronic conditions, and other related factors.

Lack of knowledge can make RLS almost impossible to be diagnosed or even recognised when seeing some medical professionals. Indeed, to some medical professionals it is almost seen as a myth, and they believe that it is a non-condition. However, it is important to note that RLS relates to poor sleep, depression, cardiovascular disease, ADHD, and even obesity; all of which comes together to contribute to the poor quality of life.

However, we (as sufferers) know that it is very real and is affecting our daily lives.

I know you can imagine going through years of misdiagnosis and a series of test just because the cause and reason for an ailment in which you suffer from is not found? This is exactly what most of us have gone through or are going through right now. Primary RLS is completely different from the secondary aspect of it. Some common phrases that sufferers have been heard to say are, 'I would cut off my own legs with a hacksaw if it would make this stop for good', or 'I want to take a hammer to my legs', or 'I just can't cope anymore!' These are those who have come to the limit of their ability to cope with the pain, isolation, depression, and social exclusion.

To RLS sufferers, even sleep is not an escape since the discomfort both prevents one from getting off to sleep, and it can also cause one to wake. Most with RLS have gone through many psychological and physical torments with little help from the medical profession because they do not understand the aetiology of the syndrome and can often put it down to being 'in the head' of the individual.

It is no wonder then, that some of us feel so desperate for help and relief, that we are willing to go so far as to take our own lives? There is some 'light at the end of the tunnel'; the toil of RLS is now being more widely shared in social media and blogs by sufferers who are sharing their experiences and supporting one another through difficult times. Many of us use this outlet as a sounding board to find understanding and relief from others such as they and to know they are not alone in their struggles. Now there are societies who are bringing awareness to the fore and scientists who are conducting research into how RLS affects sleep, function, and depression predisposing to self-harm or suicide. One such research carried out in 2019 by Zhuang *et al* studied many participants with RLS and the study showed that these individuals had a higher risk of self-harm and suicide than age- and sex-match individuals who did not have the syndrome.

Restlessness is a component of RLS. The following are some ways to overcome the feelings of restlessness. Try these tips.

Talk to someone - I advise you not to try to bottle up your emotions or try to deal with them alone. Talk to your trusted friends and family so that you can lay some of the burden off your chest. If family and friends are not an option, there are many outside agencies to whom you may talk just by phoning them. (See below).

Cry if the need arises – Do not bottle it up especially if you are a guy and live by the nonsensical orientation or mentality that 'men don't cry'. Cry it out to let off some steam, and you will be glad you did so. Don't be embarrassed because crying can ease tension and pressure and one may feel better after doing so.

Take care of yourself - Nobody knows your body better than you do, so it is left to you to take absolutely good care of yourself. Eat the right foods, drink the proper fluids, and don't abuse your intake. Rest when you need to and look after yourself with utmost care. Try some self-love and things will be much better than they were before.

Notice your feelings - As I mentioned before, you are the only one that knows your body the best. Therefore, always be aware of your feelings and moods. Know when your moods change from good to bad or vice versa. Try to banish dark thoughts and literally try to think happy thoughts. Are your feelings and thoughts becoming darker? Perhaps this is the time to ask for help.

Create time for yourself - It is not compulsory to always be with people or constantly cater for the needs and wants of others all the while neglecting what *you* need. Dedicate some time to yourself, do things that make you happy and content. Take time for yourself, treat yourself to nice things, and be grateful for your life. You can also create a ritual of taking some minutes out of every day to go somewhere quiet and relax. Do this to take care of your mental health.

Exercise - Exercise is very much taken for granted and undermined by people. In all aspects of life, having an accountability partner is something that can help you thrive and move forward. You can also join group exercise classes like Yoga or Pilates to further motivate your exercise performance. You can also do some exercises at home using a DVD or be involved in an online session. Whatever works for you; just make sure that you exercise regularly to keep you fit both mentally and physically, as well as keep you stimulated. However, do not overdo it.

Enjoy yourself - Do something you enjoy! Watch movies, have friends around, or any other thing that lightens your mood and keeps you happy. Treat yourself to a shopping spree, get a pedicure and manicure, visit the salon for a makeover, or go to the spa. The most important thing is to enjoy yourself.

See a professional - Talking to a doctor or therapist is a good place to start as this means that you are looking for ways to become a better person. Since the doctor is a professional, they can recommend other ways of coping with the restlessness felt before you become soured and perhaps take it out on someone else.

RLS patients can also experience depression at one point or another. For a diagnosis of depression, an individual needs to have experienced low mood or loss of interest in the motivational aspects of life for a minimum of two weeks. To accompany this, they have experienced at least five of the following symptoms:

- Feelings of hopelessness, sadness, or irritability almost every day.
- Lack of interest or pleasure in activities almost daily.
- Lack of appetite that result in weight loss, crucial weight loss, or a gain of five percent body weight within a month.

- Sleeping too much or too little.
- Psychomotor agitation.
- Fatigue and lack of energy daily.
- Restlessness or feelings of having 'slowed down'.
- Feelings of worthlessness or excessive and unexplained guilt almost daily.
- Difficulty in thinking clearly, concentrating, or even making habitual decisions.
- Thoughts of death, self-harm, or suicide.

If you want a self-help check list, see the *Burns depression checklist* by clicking this link here. It is a good indicator to your doctor of the severity of your depression. If you can fill one in honestly and take it to them for your consultation, it will be of great help to them in your diagnosis. It is normal for one to be completed at the start, middle and end of the monitoring of your treatment to see improvement in mood and that the medications prescribed are working.

Restless Legs Syndrome can mimic depression, as well as contribute to it. RLS was first mentioned as a disorder in 1685 when Sir Thomas Willis, an English physician wrote in his book *The London Practice of Physick*:

> *'Wherefore to some, when being abed they betake themselves to sleep, presently in the arms and legs, leapings and contractions on the tendons, and so great a restlessness and tossings of other members ensue,*

that the diseased are no more able to sleep, than if they were in a place of the greatest torture.'

Now, over three hundred years later, most people diagnosed with RLS would probably agree with this choice of explanation by Willis. Moving on to the 1800s when the first overlap of RLS with psychology happened, Theodor Wittmaack, a German neurologist, referred to this disorder as *'anxietas tibiarum'*, which can be loosely interpreted as: leg movements combined with anxiety or depression. With this description, I am sure it can be agreed that Witmaack hit the nail on the head, and this is an appropriate description of depression. Separating RLS from depression can be compared to trying to unscramble an egg, yet there are things that set them apart from each other.

RLS patients can often be misdiagnosed with depression and may be prescribed Selective Serotonin Reuptake Inhibitors (SSRIs). These are a class of drug that are usually used as antidepressants in the treatment of depressive disorder, anxiety disorders, and other psychological conditions. Others like Fluoxetine (Prozac) or Sertraline (Zoloft), can worsen the sensations of RLS; a situation which is referred to as 'augmentation'.

Approximately forty percent of people with RLS describe symptoms which present as depression when in session in the doctor's office. If there were no existence of additional RLS symptoms, it would have been quite easy to misdiagnose patients all the time.

However, has been noticed that the one-two punch of RLS and depression often strike at once. Without doubt, it can be confirmed that those with RLS also have a high risk of developing a depressive disorder than those without. Most times, the treatment will usually improve some of the symptoms of RLS. If there is the need to use antidepressant medications, non-SSRIs like Wellbutrin (Bupropion) or the Tricyclics (Imipramine, Amitriptyline, Doxepin, Amoxapine) are usually the first line of drugs prescribed by the doctor after a comprehensive health assessment.

Through the adverse effects on sleep, daytime alertness, and even energy levels, depression may be seen as being caused by RLS. Various studies on this case have illustrated that insomnia, hypersomnia, and fatigue are all independent risk factors for a major episode of depression. These are some of the few conditions associated with RLS.

These conditions in isolation are quite overwhelming, but when combined, the cumulative effects can be 'off the scale'. It would be crass of me if I told you to accept your condition, work on ways through which you can better focus your attention, live a healthy life, and keep your body in good condition. In our minds we know all of this, but we have no choice but to continue as-is until they have a breakthrough in treatment! However, as hard as it may be, do not stop going to your doctors and make yourself heard, even if you do not store much in his ability to treat your symptoms. Rather, be mindful to your rights to ask for a second opinion and referrals to places which can help.

When you do visit the doctor's office go armed with information. This is in case your GP/doctor doesn't have a first clue about treating RLS. It will show him you know more about the condition than he does, you have researched it in detail, and you are trying to do as much for yourself as you can. At least this gives the doctor the opportunity to work with you in finding a solution to your individual problem. This is especially important if your levels of depression are bringing you so low as to consider harming yourself. There is always someone who can help you get back on your feet (no pun intended). Organisations and charities are there to give expertise and take over from the GP where required, especially regarding your mental health/state of mind. I urge the reader to get help before paying the 'ultimate price' for an illness which can be managed. However, effort is required from both GP and patient.

Here is a list of some organizations which can help:

In the UK

The Samaritans – Long established volunteer organisation there to listen no matter what your concerns, worries or troubles.

Phone 116 123
Website: https://www.samaritans.org/

Community Advice and Listening Line (C.A.L.L.) - gives information and support to people experiencing mental health problem in Wales.

Phone 0800132737 (helpline),
Text HELP and your message to 8106
Website: https://callhelpline.org.uk/
Papyrus – prevention of young suicide.
Phone: 0800 068 4141
Website: https://www.papyrus-uk.org/
Sane - provides emotional support and information for anyone affected by mental health problems Website: http://www.sane.org.uk/

At the time of writing this book their website was being reorganised. The following message is on their site - leave a first name, number, and quick message on 07984 967 708 and a member of our team of trained staff and volunteers will call you back as soon as possible.

Campaign Against Living Miserably (CALM) - gives listening services, information and support for anyone who needs to talk, including a web chat

Phone: 0800585858
Website: https://www.thecalmzone.net/

Young minds – for young persons in crisis, their carers, and anyone needing help for mental health

Website: https://youngminds.org.uk/find-help/get-urgent-help/

Breathing Space - provides emotional support and assistance to people in Scotland who are depressed, in crisis or at risk of suicide. They are operating from 6 pm to 2 am.

Phone: 0800 83 85 87 Website https://breathingspace.scot/

In the US

The American Foundation for Suicide Prevention (AFSP) - The site has a lot of information regarding treatment options, resources and links for other mental health issues.

Website: https://afsp.org/find-support/resources/
Suicide Prevention Resource Centre (SPRC)
Phone: 1-800-273
Text: TALK to 8255
Website: https://www.sprc.org/

National Suicide Prevention Lifeline (the Lifeline)- Crisis workers are available 24 hours a day. Calls are free and confidential.

Phone: 1-800-273
Text: TALK to 8255
Website: https://suicidepreventionlifeline.org/talk-to-someone-now/

Suicide Awareness Voices of Education (SAVE) - helps to prevent suicide via public awareness and education, reduce the stigma or suicide ideation, and serve as a resource to those affected by suicide.

Phone: 1-800-273-8255
Website: https://save.org/

Action Alliance for Suicide Prevention - works with many groups to help understand and prevent suicide.

Website: https://theactionalliance.org/

Crisis Text Line - provides specially trained counsellors that can help individuals considering suicide or dealing with severe mental health issues in America, Canada, UK, and Ireland. There is also a text line for those not comfortable with talking

Text: HOME to 741-741 - Canada and USA

Text: 85258 - UK

Text: 50808 – Ireland

Website: https://www.crisistextline.org/

PDF of suicide prevention services - http://www.suicidehotlines.com/national.html

In Australia

Mind spot - individuals suffering from anxiety or depression.

Phone: 1800 61 44 34

Website: https://mindspot.org.au/

Beyond Blue - individuals feeling depressed or anxious

Phone: 1300 22 4636 or chat online.

Website: https://www.beyondblue.org.au/

Lifeline - individuals experiencing a crisis or thinking about suicide

Phone: 13 11 14 or chat online.

Website: https://www.lifeline.org.au/

Suicide Call Back Service - individuals thinking about suicide

Phone: 1300 659 467.

Website: https://www.suicidecallbackservice.org.au/

In Canada

Canada Suicide Prevention Service

Website: https://www.crisisservicescanada.ca/en/

Suicide.org – pdf list of services in Canada

Website: http://www.suicide.org/hotlines/international/canada-suicide-hotlines.html

CONCLUSION

'RLS is one of the most common sleep and movement disorders affecting about 5% of U.S. adults.'

Dr. Xiang Gao of the Pennsylvania state University College of Medicine in University Park.

(NICE cite that the prevalence of RLS in UK, US and Europe is around 5 – 10 %.)

I have discussed how Restless Legs Syndrome affects our everyday lives throughout the pages of this book. Sadly, it is still a very much misunderstood area in medicine and many doctors are unsure of how to treat it. It becomes furthermore difficult when the aspect of augmentation raises its head. However, there are ongoing studies into this Syndrome with some interesting findings about the aetiology of the syndrome. Doctors have discovered that low levels of iron within the brain and body may have an impact on controlling the symptoms of RLS. Other minerals also play a large part in ensuring symptoms are controlled as best they can be. They are learning more and are understanding more about how to treat it. With any luck, one day they will be able to find a cure. We can only hope.

Sadly, the syndrome can also be a part of other chronic illness such as Fibromyalgia and liver disease, to name only two, and as such, the medications used to help these illnesses may cause an exacerbation of RLS. It can be a vicious circle. Even some of the medications used to help control RLS can cause the symptoms to become worse! This is where we ourselves must become experts in the syndrome so we can show the doctors that we are capable of researching and doing as much as we can to understand that from which we suffer. We are then able, in some circumstances, to guide them into making appropriate decisions about treatment and referrals. Doctors today, are generally more geared into working with the patient instead of against and are mostly at least willing to listen to what we have learned and accept that we know more. After all, they have so much else to be aware of and we are only one very small cog in a vast wheel. We do, however, have the right to a second opinion and even to change our doctor's services if the current practitioner is not willing to engage and help.

It is also important to remember that the symptoms one person suffers from RLS, may not be the same as another person's but we all become fatigued and exhausted from the lack of sleep caused by our dancing, jittery, and painful legs. I know the symptoms I display are not the same as someone else's, but that does not take away that each of our experiences are important to each individual and their effects are just as devastating whether your legs jump and jitter or are just consistently painful and uncomfortable. I need a comparable solution to this, just as much as you do!

We must also remember that although 'we' may be coping reasonably well with our symptoms, others may not, and they may be heading downwards with Mr Churchill's 'black dog' watching over them and leading them into depression and dark thoughts.

However, we carry on, because we must for our family, lovers, jobs and more importantly – ourselves.

I hope that you have enjoyed reading this book and may even have found some useful tips within the pages of this book and maybe some humour too. As I said, I am only an expert on the subject because I suffer from it. I don't have a fancy doctorate. I am a graduate of the University of Life, but I want to try to help those like myself by passing on the information I have discovered about RLS.

I am fully aware some of the tips will not work for you, but I hope they have given you some ideas for treatments you may want to pursue, and perhaps, like me, have gained insight into treatments you have never even heard of. If I have prompted you to go and try some, I am very happy with that.

I was not aware of the potency and promise of the use of essential oils and aromatherapy treatment. I took great delight in playing with these, and I really did play. I bought books about their use, all the carrier oils mentioned and bottles and spray bottles to put the blends in. A room atomiser has been an absolute life saver particularly when I have felt low and sad needing a 'pick-me-up'. I have had fun with them although I have found that Eucalyptus oil on the filter of my vacuum cleaner, is not a good idea. It does not leave the pleasant after-cleaning odour I had in mind! Maybe, something else here will really spark your interest and lead you on a journey of discovery.

If you enjoyed this book, you could do well to leave a review on Audible or Amazon and please, do feel free to recommend it to your friends, particularly if they suffer from RLS.

For further information and upcoming books, please email me at: lisa@ljhudson98.com

FURTHER READING

If you wish to learn more about this condition and dive deeper into the medical aspect of it, here are some further sites which you may find informative and interesting.

RLS Foundation - rls.org
RLS-UK - https://www.rls-uk.org/
RLS UK – Facebook Group - https://www.facebook.com/RLSUK
My RLS Monitor ™- https://www.rls-uk.org/rls-monitor
Southern California RLS Support Group - http://rlshelp.org/
The Sleep Foundation - https://www.sleepfoundation.org/restless-legs-syndrome/treatment

Facebook Groups

Restless Legs Syndrome (RLS) Worldwide Support Group – https://www.facebook.com/groups/1211622138929365

Restless Legs Syndrome (UK Support Group) – https://www.facebook.com/groups/302984673467796

Restless Legs Syndrome App Group – https://www.facebook.com/groups/restlesslegssyndromeapp

Restless Legs Syndrome (RLS) Support Group – https://www.facebook.com/groups/260313314437979

LJ Hudson's Restless Legs Support Community https://www.facebook.com/Lisa-Hudsons-Restless-Legs-Support-Community-111993997817607

RESOURCE PAGE

1. *11 Best Home Remedies To Treat Restless Leg Syndrome*. (2020, February 24). How to Cure. https://howtocure.com/natural-treatments-restless-legs-syndrome#:~:text=Meditation%20and%20exercises%20that%20involve%20deep%20inhalation%20 and,daily%20basis%20every%20morning%20on%20an%20empty%20stomach
2. Allen, Phd, R., Becker, MD, P. M., Brogan, MD, FCCP, R., Schmidt MD, PhD, M., Kushida MD, PhD, C. A., Fry, MD, PhD, J. M., Poceta MD, J. S., & Winslow, MD, D. (2004). Ropinirole decreases periodic leg movements and improves sleep parameters in patients with restless legs 40.syndrome. *Sleep*, *27*(5), 907–914. https://doi.org/10.1093/sleep/27.5.907

3. Ambardekar,MD, N. (2020, December 13). *Treatments for Restless Legs Syndrome*. WebMD. https://www.webmd.com/brain/restless-legs-syndrome/restless-leg-syndrome-treatment
4. Aukerman, M. M., Aukerman, D., Baysrd, M., Tudiver, F., Thorp, L., & Bailey, B. (2006). Exercise and restless legs syndrome: a randomized control trial. *Journal of the American Board of Family Medicine, 19*(5), 487–493. https://doi.org/10.3122/jabfm19.5.487
5. Avni, T., Reich, S., Lev, N., & Gafter-Gvili, A. (2019). Iron supplementation for restless legs syndrome -A systematic review and meta-analysis. *European Journal of Internal Medicine, 63,* 34–41. https://doi.org/10.1016/j.ejim.2019.02.009
6. Beckerman, MD,FACC, J. (2019, September 4). *High Blood Pressure and Calcium Channel Blockers*. WebMD. https://www.webmd.com/hypertension-high-blood-pressure/guide/treatment-calcium-channel
7. Brodeur, C., Montplaisir, J., Godbout, R., & Marinier, R. (1988). . Treatment of restless legs syndrome and periodic movements during sleep with L-dopa:a double-blind, controlled study. *Neurology, 38*(12), 1845. https://doi.org/10.1212/WNL.38.12.1845
8. Brogan, D. (2017, January 14). *PLMD: Do Your*

Limb's 'Jerk' And Move Involuntary? RLS-UK. https://www.rls-uk.org/news/plmd

9. Burns, D. D. (1989). The Burns Depression Checklist. *The Feelig Good Handbook*. Published. https://www.fspcares.org/wp-content/uploads/2020/03/Burns-Checklists.pdf
10. Cara, D., Manisha, W., & Lonnie, Z. (2012). Iron's role in paediatric restless legs syndrome-a review. Paediatrics Child Health, 17(4), 193-197. doi: 10.1093/pch/17.4.193
11. Cassoobhoy, MD, MPH, A. (2020, July 2). *Iron Deficiency Anemia*. WebMD. https://www.webmd.com/a-to-z-guides/iron-deficiency-anemia
12. Chen, J. M., Chiu, P. F., Chang, Y. J., Jun, Y., Hsu, P. C., Chang, C. C., & Lo, L. C. (2020). Effect of electroacupuncture on restless legs syndrome (RLS) in hemodialysis patients A protocol for systematic review and meta-analysis. *Medicine, 99*(50). https://doi.org/10.1097/MD.0000000000023629
13. Cotter, P. E., & O'Keeffe, S. T. (2006). Restless leg syndrome: is it a real problem? *Therapeutics and Clinical Risk Management, 2*(4), 465–475. https://doi.org/10.2147/tcrm.2006.2.4.465
14. Deevoy, R. (2021, August 11). *14 best CBD oils to boost your mood, aid relaxation and help manage pain*. Independent. https://www.independent.co.uk/

extras/indybest/best-cbd-oil-uk-benefits-b1827972.html

15. *Exercise.* (n.d.). National Health Service. Retrieved 2 August 2021, from https://www.nhs.uk/live-well/exercise/
16. Ferguson, G., & Ware W.A. (2015). Sleep, pain and cannabis. *Journal for Sleep Disorders and Therapy,* 4(2), 1000191. doi: 10.41722167-0277.1000191
17. Gao, X., Schwarzschild, M. A., Wang, H., & Ascherio, A. (2009). Obesity and restless legs syndrome in men and women. *Neurology, 72*(14), 1255–1261. https://doi.org/10.1212/01.wnl.0000345673.35676.1c
18. Garcia-Borreguero, D. (2020, November). *Augmentation – a potential complication of drug treatment*. NICE.Org.Uk. https://cks.nice.org.uk/topics/restless-legs-syndrome/prescribing-information/augmentation/
19. HORIZANT - gabapentin encarbil tablet, extended release [Comment on the article "Drug label information"]. (2021, August 19). *Daily Med.* https://dailymed.nlm.nih.gov/dailymed/drugInfo.cfm?setid=4c486fc7-c8c4-4c6c-b30c-366dabaeaadd
20. Innes, K., Selfe, T., Agarwal, P., Williams, K., & Flack, K. L. (2013). Efficacy of an eight-week yoga intervention on symptoms of restless legs syndrome (RLS): A pilot study. *The Journal of Alternative and*

Complementary Medicine, 19(6), 527–535. https://doi.org/10.1089/acm.2012.0330

21. John Hopkins Medicine. (n.d.-a). *Causes of Restless Legs Syndrome*. Hopkinsmedicine.Org. Retrieved 2 August 2021, from https://www.hopkinsmedicine.org/neurology_neurosurgery/centers_clinics/restless-legs-syndrome/what-is-rls/causes.html
22. John Hopkins Medicine. (n.d.-b). *Natural Sleep Aids: Home Remedies to Help You Sleep*. Retrieved 2 August 2021, from https://www.hopkinsmedicine.org/health/wellness-and-prevention/natural-sleep-aids-home-remedies-to-help-you-sleep
23. Killgore, W. D. S. (2010). *Effects of sleep deprivation on cognition*. Science Direct. https://www.sciencedirect.com/science/article/pii/B9780444537027000075
24. Kubala MS, RD, J. (2018, February 26). *7 Benefits and Uses of CBD Oil (Plus Side Effects)*. Healthline. https://www.healthline.com/nutrition/cbd-oil-benefits
25. LaMattina, J. (2019, September 4). Suicide Risk For Restless Legs Syndrome Patients. *Forbes*. https://www.forbes.com/sites/johnlamattina/2019/09/04/suicide-risk-for-restless-legs-syndrome-patients/?sh=233ef6605f27
26. Lange, D. (2021, March 4). *Cycling - Statistics &*

Facts. Statista. https://www.statista.com/topics/1686/cycling/#topicHeader__wrapper

27. Mandal,MD, A. (2019, April 9). *What is Dopamine?* Medical Life Sciences. https://www.news-medical.net/health/What-is-Dopamine.aspx
28. Mawer, MSc, CISSN, R. (2020, February 28). *17 Proven Tips to Sleep Better at Night*. Healthline. https://www.healthline.com/nutrition/17-tips-to-sleep-better
29. Mayo Clinic Staff. (n.d.). *Restless legs syndrome*. Mayo Clinic. Retrieved 2 August 2021, from https://www.mayoclinic.org/diseases-conditions/restless-legs-syndrome/symptoms-causes/syc-20377168
30. Megelin, T., & Ghorayeb I. (2017). Cannabis for restless legs syndrome: a report of six patients. *Sleep Medicine*, 36,182-183. https://doi.org/10.1016/j.sleep.2017.04.019
31. Miller, R. M. (2016, December 3). *17 Powerful Essential Oils For Restless Leg Syndrome*. UpNature. https://upnature.com/blogs/news/17-powerful-essential-oils-for-restless-leg-syndrome
32. Mind. (n.d.). *Supporting someone who feels suicidal*. Mind.Org.Uk. Retrieved 2 August 2021, from https://www.mind.org.uk/information-support/helping-someone-else/supporting-someone-who-feels-suicidal/useful-contacts/
33. MIRAPEX- pramipexole dihydrochloride tablet

[Comment on the article "Drug Label Information"]. (2021, July 1). *Daily Med.* https://dailymed.nlm.nih.gov/dailymed/drugInfo.cfm?setid=688fa4d7-de12-4930-8bc5-0169297c1da6

34. MIRAPEX-ER - pramipexole dihydrochloride tablet, extended release [Comment on the article "Drug Label information"]. (2021, July 20). *Daily Med.* https://dailymed.nlm.nih.gov/dailymed/drugInfo.cfm?setid=e2902ed1-cfeb-4815-adc3-129c577917a1
35. Mitchell, U. (2010). Use of near-infrared light to reduce symptoms associated with restless legs syndrome in a woman: a case report. *Journal of Medical Case Reports, 4,* 286. https://doi.org/10.1186/1752-1947-4-286
36. Mitchell, U. (2015). Medical devices for restless legs syndrome-clinical utility of the relaxis pad. *Therapeutics and Clinical Risk Management, 11,* 1789–1794. https://doi.org/10.2147/TCRM.S87208
37. Mitchell, U., Myrere, J. W., Johnson, A., & Hilton, S. C. (2010). Restless legs near syndrome and near-infrared light: an alternative option. *Physiotherapy Theory and Practices, 27*(5), 345–351. https://doi.org/10.3109/09593985.2010.511440
38. Murray, A. (2016, January 13). *Homemade Restless Leg Spray + How To Make Magnesium Oil.* Omnomally.Com. https://omnomally.com/2016/01/

13/homemade-restless-leg-spray-how-to-make-magnesium-oil/

39. Nair, R., & Maseeh, A. (2012). Vitamin D: The "sunshine" vitamin. *Journal of Pharmacology & Pharmacotherapeutics, 3*(2), 118–126. https://doi.org/10.4103/0976-500X.95506
40. NEUPRO - rotigotine patch, extended release [Comment on the article "Drug Label Information"]. (2021, July 1). *Daily Med.* https://dailymed.nlm.nih.gov/dailymed/drugInfo.cfm?setid=939e28c5-f3a9-42c0-9a2d-8d471d82a6e0
41. NICE. (2020, November). *Restless Legs Syndrome: How Common is it?* Nice.Org. https://cks.nice.org.uk/topics/restless-legs-syndrome/background-information/prevalence/#:~:text=Prognosis-,How%20common%20is%20it%3F,of%20adults%20in%20northern%20Europe.
42. Office of Communications and Public Liaison National Institute of Neurological Disorders and Stroke. (2017, May). *Restless Legs Syndrome Fact Sheet.* National Institute of Neurological Disorders and Stroke. https://www.ninds.nih.gov/Disorders/Patient-Caregiver-Education/Fact-Sheets/Restless-Legs-Syndrome-Fact-Sheet
43. *Relieve Leg Pain & Get Moving!* (n.d.). Revitive. Retrieved 2 August 2021, from https://www.revitive.com/us

44. REQUIP - ropinirole tablet film coated [Comment on the article "Highlights of prescribing information"]. (2021, July 1). *Daily Med*. https://dailymed.nlm.nih.gov/dailymed/drugInfo.cfm?setid=de0bb94f-4fd8-4f27-5ba6-6f392dd5160f
45. Resnick Neuropsychiatric Hospital. (n.d.). *Checklist for Depression*. Uclahealth.Org. Retrieved 2 August 2021, from https://www.uclahealth.org/resnick/checklist-for-depression
46. Rezaeian, M., Rad, H. S., Mostafavi, S. A., Fathinejad, A., Ranjbar, E., & Bidaki, R. (2014). Prevalence of sleep disorders in medical internship students of Rafsanjan University of Medical Sciences. *Int J clin surg adv, 2*(4), 74-81.
47. RLS-UK. (n.d.). *WHAT IS RLS?* Retrieved 2 August 2021, from https://www.rls-uk.org/
48. Roche, D. (2021, February 11). *Do You Have Vitamin B12 Deficiency?* Let's Get Checked. https://www.letsgetchecked.com/articles/do-you-have-vitamin-b12-deficiency/?imp=cpc&gclid=EAIaIQobChMI4ovSqZ7H8QIVTNPtCh28NAUwEAAYASAAEgItbfD_BwE
49. Russel, M. (2007). Massage therapy and restless legs syndrome. *Journal of Body Work and Movement Therapies, 11*(2), 146–150. https://doi.org/10.1016/j.jbmt.2006.12.00
50. Russell, M. (2011). Massage therapy and restless legs

syndrome. *Journal of Bodywork and Movement Therapies, 15*(2), 253. https://doi.org/10.1016/j.jbmt.2006.12.001

51. Saraj, W., Samah, A., Bahaa, A., Iman, R., Badr, A., Moaiyyad, K., & Mohamed, H. (2018). The association between vitamin D level and restless legs syndrome: A population-based case-control study. .. *Journal of Clinical Sleep Medicine, 14*(4), 557–564. https://doi.org/10.5664/jcsm.7044
52. Sarma, G. R. K., Arvin, N. P., Meghana, S., Thomas, M., & Raghunandan, N. (2018). Restless legs syndrome as an early neurological manifestation of vitamin B12 deficiency. *International Journal of Neurology and Neurosurgery, 10*(3), 161–167. https://doi.org/10.21088/ijnns.0975.0223.10318.4
53. Sheng, MD, Z., Na, PhD,MHS, M., & Winkelman, MD,PhD, J. W. (2019, August 23). *Association of Restless Legs Syndrome With Risk of Suicide and Self-harm.* Jama Network. https://jamanetwork.com/journals/jamanetworkopen/fullarticle/2748664
54. Sleep-Disorders.net. (2020, March 30). *Does Near-Infrared Light Therapy Help RLS Symptoms?* https://restlesslegssyndrome.sleep-disorders.net/living/near-infrared-light-therapy
55. Smith, MA, M., Robinson, L., & Segal, MA, R. (2020, October). *Restless Legs Syndrome (RLS).*

Helpguide.Org. https://www.helpguide.org/articles/sleep/restless-leg-syndrome-rls.htm#

56. Smith, MA, M., Robinson, L., & Segal, MA, R. (2021, June). *How to Sleep Better*. Helpguide.Org. https://www.helpguide.org/articles/sleep/getting-better-sleep.htm
57. Spritzler, F. (2021, June 15). *8 Signs and Symptoms of Vitamin D Deficiency*. Healthline.Com. https://www.healthline.com/nutrition/vitamin-d-deficiency-symptoms#_noHeaderPrefixedContent
58. The Bark Team. (2020, January 15). *Top 10 Suicide Prevention Organisations and Resources*. The Bark Blog. https://www.bark.us/blog/top-10-suicide-prevention-resources/
59. *Treatment: Restless Legs Syndrome*. (n.d.). NHS. Retrieved 2 August 2021, from https://www.nhs.uk/conditions/restless-legs-syndrome/treatment/
60. Ventuno Yoga. (2018, November 1). *8 Easy Yoga Poses to Calm Restless Legs Syndrome* [Video]. YouTube https://www.youtube.com/channel/UC_xYALq063ZWm-26IeG9cCQ
61. Wali, S., Shukr, A., Boudal, A., Alsaiari, A., & Krayem, A. (2015).). The effect of vitamin D supplements on the severity of restless legs syndrome. *Sleep & Breathing, 19*(2), 579–583. https://doi.org/10.1007/s11325-014-1049-y
62. Weidong, P., Wang, M., Mao, L., Wang, Q., Kwak, S.,

Jiang, W., & Yamamoto, Y. (2015). Actigraph evaluation of acupuncture for treating restless legs syndrome. *Evidence-Based Complementary and Alternative Medicine (ECAM)*. Published. https://doi.org/10.1155/2015/343201

63. *Welcome to Sahaja Yoga Meditation UK*. (n.d.). Sahaja Yoga Meditation UK. Retrieved 19 August 2021, from https://www.sahajayogalondon.co.uk/what-is-yoga/
64. Zell, K. (n.d.). *How Compression Socks can Help Ease the Symptoms of Restless Leg Syndrome*. Ames Walker. Retrieved 19 August 2021, from https://www.ameswalker.com/blogs/news/how-compression-socks-can-help-ease-the-symptoms-of-restless-leg-syndrome

Printed in Great Britain
by Amazon

81846653R00109